More Praise for *How to Reach & Teach English Language Learners*

"One of the single most urgent questions facing educators today is, 'How can we best identify and meet the needs of English language learners?' With a depth of practical experience, coupled with action research to identify high-impact strategies for engaging English language learners, this book presents a hands-on approach for all educators who provide instruction to students acquiring a second language."

—Armene Chavdarian, retired deputy superintendent, Instructional Services, El Monte City School District, El Monte, California

"Rachel Carrillo Syrja has written a comprehensive guide on second language learners that should be on every educator's reading list. Not only does Rachel look at specific instructional strategies, she also provides powerful insight into assessment, grading, and cultural aspects of teaching ELLs."

—Christopher Hanson, professional development associate, The Leadership and Learning Center

How to Reach & Teach English Language Learners

Jossey-Bass Teacher

Jossey-Bass Teacher provides educators with practical knowledge and tools to create a positive and lifelong impact on student learning. We offer classroom-tested and research-based teaching resources for a variety of grade levels and subject areas. Whether you are an aspiring, new, or veteran teacher, we want to help you make every teaching day your best.

From ready-to-use classroom activities to the latest teaching framework, our value-packed books provide insightful, practical, and comprehensive materials on the topics that matter most to K–12 teachers. We hope to become your trusted source for the best ideas from the most experienced and respected experts in the field.

Titles in the Jossey-Bass Teacher
Reach and Teach Series

How to Reach and Teach Children with Challenging Behavior:
Practical, Ready-to-Use Interventions That Work

Kaye Otten and Jodie Tuttle • ISBN 978-0-470-50516-8

How to Reach and Teach Children with ADD/ADHD:
Practical Techniques, Strategies, and Interventions, Second Edition

Sandra F. Rief • ISBN 978-0-7879-7295-0

How to Reach and Teach Children and Teens with Dyslexia

Cynthia M. Stowe • ISBN 978-0-13-032018-6

How to Reach and Teach All Children in the Inclusive Classroom:
Practical Strategies, Lessons, and Activities, Second Edition

Sandra F. Rief and Julie A. Heimburge • ISBN 978-0-7879-8154-9

How to Reach and Teach All Children Through Balanced Literacy:
User-Friendly Strategies, Tools, Activities, and Ready-to-Use Materials

Sandra F. Rief and Julie A. Heimburge • ISBN 978-0-7879-8805-0

How to Reach & Teach English Language Learners

Rachel Carrillo Syrja

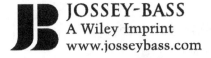

JOSSEY-BASS
A Wiley Imprint
www.josseybass.com

Published by Jossey-Bass
A Wiley Imprint
989 Market Street, San Francisco, CA 94103-1741—www.josseybass.com

Jossey-Bass books and products are available through most bookstores. To contact Jossey-Bass directly call our Customer Care Department within the U.S. at 800-956-7739, outside the U.S. at 317-572-3986, or fax 317-572-4002.

Jossey-Bass also publishes its books in a variety of electronic formats. Some content that appears in print may not be available in electronic books.

Library of Congress Cataloging-in-Publication Data
Syrja, Rachel Carrillo, 1968-
　　How to reach and teach English language learners / Rachel Carrillo Syrja.—1st ed.
　　　　p. cm.—(J-B ed : reach and teach ; 4)
　　Includes bibliographical references and index.
　　ISBN 978-0-470-76761-0 (pbk.)
　　ISBN 978-1-118-09815-8 (ebk.)
　　ISBN 978-1-118-09816-5 (ebk.)
　　ISBN 978-1-118-09817-2 (ebk.)
　1.　English language -Study and teaching—Foreign speakers.　I. Title.　II. Title: How to reach and teach English language learners.
　PE1128.A2S97 2011
　428.0071—dc23

2011021313

Printed in the United States of America
FIRST EDITION
PB Printing　　10 9 8 7 6 5 4

About the Author

Rachel Carrillo Syrja, M.Ed., is a professional development associate with the Leadership and Learning Center in Denver, Colorado. A native Spanish speaker raised in a bilingual household and a veteran educator of English as a Second Language (ESL) and Title I students, she has placed a strong emphasis on serving English Language Learners throughout her career.

During her nearly two decades in education, Syrja has worked as a classroom teacher, mathematics resource teacher, and professional developer. Her varied educational experiences as well as leadership roles have enhanced her knowledge and skills in the areas of curriculum, instruction, and assessment. Among her many leadership roles, she has designed and implemented districtwide staff development in the areas of English language development, working with struggling readers, standards-based education, and assessment for learning. In addition, she has conducted workshops for teachers and administrators on data teams, professional learning communities, and using assessment data to drive instruction, and she has presented at national conferences such as ASCD.

Throughout her career, Syrja has led and facilitated district task forces for curriculum adoptions, standards-based report cards, and the creation of benchmark assessments and pacing guides. She recently developed and implemented an ESL curriculum for a large urban school district, and her current focus is on ensuring a high degree of implementation of professional development initiatives.

About The Leadership and Learning Center

The Leadership and Learning Center provides world-class, research-based professional development services and solutions for educators who serve students from pre-kindergarten through college. The Center has worked in all fifty states and every Canadian province, as well as Europe, Africa, Asia, South America, and the Middle East. The Center works with public schools, religious and secular independent schools, charter schools, community colleges, technical schools, universities, state departments of education, and international education associations. Center Professional Development Associates are experienced superintendents, administrators, and educators who provide comprehensive practices for clients in the areas of standards, assessment, instruction, accountability, data analysis, and leadership.

Acknowledgments

I begin by thanking those individuals in my life who had a profound impact on the writing of this book: first and foremost, my parents, Alfonso and Florentina, who taught my brothers and me the importance and value of an education, and my beloved brothers, Martin and Alfonso, with whom I spent the happiest of childhoods.

I offer thanks as well to my incredibly forward-thinking administrators Barbara Gera, Armene Chavdarian, Cynthia Traino, and Jeff Seymour, who had the wisdom to know the importance of developing the knowledge base of their team in all curricular areas, and particularly in strategies for supporting English learner populations; to Guy DeRosa, Jessica Pardini, and Shirley Burkhardt for always challenging me to continue learning and growing; and to the administrators, teachers, and students of the city of El Monte, California, who never fail to inspire me.

There are times in one's life when the stars align and unexpected opportunities present themselves to you. The Leadership and Learning Center entered my life in 2004 and literally changed the trajectory of my career. Special thanks go to Douglas Reeves and Larry Ainsworth for believing in me and in my ability to write this book and to the amazing professional development associates there, including Bonnie Bishop, Juan Cordova, Mary Vedra, Lisa Almeida, Loan Mascorro, Angela Peery, Linda Gregg, Steve Ventura, and Connie Kamm, without whose professional guidance and support this book would have never happened. Special thanks go to Kristin Anderson, who has supported and encouraged me to continue challenging myself and to always be the author of my own story.

I extend a very special word of appreciation to the editorial staff at Jossey-Bass, including Marjorie McAneny and Robin Lloyd, for their tireless support. And to my editor, Beverly Miller, whose countless hours of editing have made my work sound better than I ever imagined it could.

To my husband, Randy, whose love and devotion carried me through the writing of every word in this book, I offer countless thanks. Finally, my daughter, Haley, withstood countless hours without her mother's company and always did so without a single complaint. I cherish every moment I get to spend with you!

Contents

PART THREE

REACHING ENGLISH LANGUAGE LEARNERS

PART FOUR
TEACHING ENGLISH LANGUAGE LEARNERS

PART FIVE

TEACHING STRATEGIES ACROSS THE CONTENT AREAS

PART SIX

PUTTING THESE PRACTICES TO WORK

For my beautiful Haley.

Preface

The families of English language learners come to us with the yearning, hope, and promise of America—families like my own who emigrated to the United States from Mexico and raised their children in a bilingual, bicultural household where Spanish was the primary language.

My story is not unlike those of many of the students currently sitting in your classrooms. It begins with a nineteen-year-old young woman who came to the United States in 1962 from a rural village in Mexico. Not only did my mother bring with her the hopes and dreams that so many other immigrants come with, but she also brought the steady strength and courage that comes from surviving extreme hardship and poverty. With her hair in two long braids and wrapped in the safety of her *rebozo* (a long woven scarf worn over the head and shoulders by Spanish and Mexican women), she arrived in the United States and faced an alien world filled with wonders that were totally new to her. She would later tell us about her amazement at things so many of us take for granted, like running water and electricity. Her first attempt at communicating resulted in her walking away, frustrated, after imagining that Americans must surely be deaf because they could not understand her.

My father, a twenty-one-year-old third-generation Mexican American, has told the story of the first moment he laid eyes on this beautiful, traditionally dressed young woman and how in that moment he knew he would marry her. True to my father's wish, the two married a year later. And so began their unlikely story—unlikely because of the seemingly insurmountable challenges they both faced in realizing the American dream. My father had barely an eighth-grade education, and my mother had been allowed to attend school only through the second grade in Mexico. Despite their limited education and my mother's lack of English, they persevered through hard work and an undying belief in the idea that if they worked hard enough, anything was possible. It was historically a time wrought with struggle and promise, and perhaps it was this promise that fueled their dreams.

They settled in southern California and raised my two brothers and me to believe that we could achieve anything we wanted in life and that the secret to our success was having a college education. My father also recognized an opportunity in our bilingualism, and so he and my mother encouraged and nurtured the two languages. My father hoped, often out loud, that armed with a college education and two languages, his children would never have to toil as he and my mother did for so much of their lives in order to reach their dreams.

My eighteen years in education all took place in the same town where I was born and raised, a town that experienced tremendous demographic changes during the late 1970s and 1980s. It evolved from predominantly white, suburban, and middle class to a town of immigrants. First to arrive were the immigrants from Mexico and Central America, followed shortly by a wave of Vietnamese, Cambodian, Chinese, and Filipino. It was a town in the midst of growth and changing demographics, the same growth and change that has since taken place in other states around the country.

Like the rest of us, I am the sum of my experiences. Growing up with Spanish as my primary language until I went to school, living in a bicultural home, and teaching English language learners my entire career have greatly influenced me. What has perhaps influenced me most is having been raised by loving parents who sacrificed so much in order to ensure that their children would have a better life than they did.

Their dreams for their children are not unlike those of every immigrant who comes to the United States. Although the current climate in this country may not feel so full of promise as it was in the early 1960s, behind every immigrant child are parents with the same resolve for a bright future for their children. Our challenge is to ensure that all of these children have every opportunity to realize their potential. Like my parents, I believe that education holds the key to unlocking the promise behind every child who enters our classrooms.

How to Reach &
Teach English
Language Learners

Introduction

The past decade has seen vast changes in the field of education that have included an explosion in information and resources. This book is not meant to add yet one more thing to do to already overly burdened teachers, but rather to provide an opportunity for reflection and conversation in the service of seeking answers. Within the pages that follow, you will find valuable information about the challenges we face when teaching English learners, as well as practical strategies that can help us meet those challenges.

There is a common saying in teaching that I learned early in my career. I clearly remember fretting over a visit by the district superintendent and worrying out loud whether my classroom would meet his expectations. I was particularly worried about my implementation of a district initiative when one of my more experienced colleagues said to me, "This too shall pass." In fact, I heard those same words several times during my first few years as a classroom teacher. Most of the time, they were correct, but there came a time when the saying no longer held true.

It was 1996, and I had just returned from a conference where I'd heard about academic standards and an accompanying accountability system that would turn the field of education on its head. As I was relaying this information to my teacher colleagues, I quickly realized that they had not received this information with the same sense of urgency with which it had been relayed to me, and before long I heard it again: "Rachel, Rachel, this too shall pass!"

Thirteen years later I can say with certainty that they were wrong. Many of them have since retired, still holding fast to their principled belief that like everything else in education, standards and accountability would come and go. It has not, and I believe it never should. At its best, accountability has forced us to become data driven and reflective upon the practices we implement and the impact they've had on student learning. At its worst, its led schools on a wild goose chase for a silver bullet, resulting in an endless number of initiatives being pursued at school sites across the county, oftentimes with frustratingly few results.

Standards and accountability are here to stay, and we are bombarded with endless initiatives promising to help us meet those standards and rigorous measures of accountability. They come and go almost as quickly as the saying can be uttered: "This too shall pass!"

Amid this confusion, I hope to provide in this book an opportunity for teachers to take stock of what they are doing so that they can reflect on their practice and find ways to improve it.

Where Are the Answers?

In doing the research for this book, I originally set out with the purpose of finding answers. Surely, I thought, some great yet undiscovered pearls of wisdom lay somewhere on a dusty shelf waiting for me to find them. Unfortunately, it didn't take long for me to realize that sadly this wasn't the case. Although there are bodies of research and endless titles promising to hold the secret to success for English language learners, there truly is no one answer for all of them. I hope to provide the inspiration for you to take the information in this book and apply it in a way that helps you discover your own answers. After all, that is what teaching is all about: using the tools that allow each of us to use our professional judgment to apply them in a way that yields success in our own situations.

Using This Resource

The chapters in Part One address the current state of education for English learners and make the case for urgency. The issue of long-term English language learners is discussed as well as possible solutions to this fast-growing population.

Part Two is designed to help classroom teachers, schools, and districts take a moment to reflect on their existing English language learner (ELL) programs and assess the effectiveness of the practices currently in place.

Part Three reinforces the importance of connecting with the families of our English language learners and using what we learn about them to help us develop a more culturally responsive curriculum.

Building on clarity with regard to ELL programs, the chapters in Part Four focus on teachers—without a doubt, the most important factor in the education of our children. In fact, quantifiable research now confirms what we had long suspected: what teachers do matters.

Part Five is filled with research-based strategies in all content areas that teachers in K–12 can implement with confidence. My intention is to offer what the research has found on what works with ELLs, along with a variety of strategies for diverse populations of varying grade and language acquisition levels.

The final chapter, in Part Six, provides practical ideas for implementing these strategies in a way that works for each individual school, classroom, teacher, and student. Although some elements of these strategies must remain constant, it is also important for teachers to differentiate the strategies in ways that make them most effective for their own students.

Part One

English Language Learners

The chapters in Part One investigate recent demographic trends and their effect on instruction for English language learners (ELLs). These trends have led to some major challenges that have increased the urgency for improving instruction for these students. With the increased numbers of ELLs being placed in mainstream classes has come a new designation: long-term English learners. Part One ends by exploring the causes of and possible solutions for this trend and a closer look at how students acquire language.

Chapter 1

The Current State of Education for English Language Learners

In This Chapter

- The changing demographics for ELLs
- The importance of best practices
- The significant impact that degree of implementation has on student achievement
- How long it takes to acquire English
- Characteristics of the new and growing population of English learners

Despite many opinions to the contrary, numerous recent research studies have made clear that the classroom teacher is the most influential factor in student achievement.[1] At a time when the number of English language learners (ELLs) in classrooms is increasing dramatically, we are in desperate need of research into what works specifically with these students. States across the nation are facing growing numbers of English learners, in places that have traditionally had high numbers of English learners and places that have not. As of 2004–2005, the following states and territories had the largest number of ELLs:[2]

California 1,591,525
Texas   684,007
Puerto Rico 578,534
Florida   299,346
New York   203,583
Arizona   155,789
Illinois   192,764

The projections for the population show that this demographic will continue to grow.

What Works with ELLs

In their landmark 1997 research, Wayne Thomas and Virginia Collier made the case for long-term research into what works for ELLs.[3] The urgency of that study has not diminished today. Collier and Thomas also brought to light the fact that long-term studies into program efficacy for ELLs need to take place. In fact, their findings show that while in the short term some practices show promising results, these very practices prove detrimental in the later years of an ELL's educational career. They also remind us to not judge a program's efficacy based on its label, but rather on the actual content of that label.

Over the course of my career, I have had the opportunity to visit K–12 rural, suburban, and inner-city classrooms across the country. As a result of what I have seen and learned, I want to challenge a couple of previously held opinions. In my eighteen years of working in a suburban school district with high levels of poverty and students for whom English was a second language, I developed the notion that our students and their needs were unique. I would listen suspiciously to researchers or authorities in education who would propose strategies and ideas that had worked in other districts across the country. My answer always was, "Sure that may have worked in that school or district, but our students are different and I don't think we can assume it would work here." While my instincts were partially correct, they were also partially mistaken.

The one thing I have witnessed in classroom after classroom, state after state, rural and urban populations alike, is that good teaching strategies work everywhere. But I have also seen good teaching strategies fail in classrooms where the teacher has not taken into account the needs of the students and has not differentiated the instruction appropriately for the group of students in front of her. So while the teacher may be using the strategy, the fact that student needs have not been accounted for affects the degree of implementation. Full implementation would mean that the strategy is being implemented at the highest degree and is being appropriately differentiated for the students. We know from research that the element that matters most is degree of implementation. In fact, Doug Reeves has found in study after study that while we may assume that results increase with each incremental

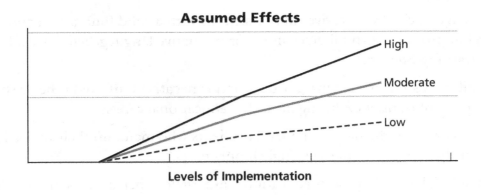

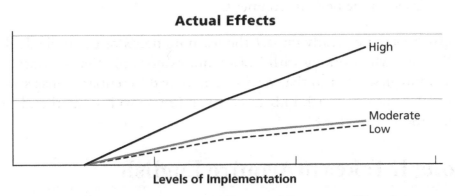

Figure 1.1 Assumed and Actual Effects of Degree of Implementation

Source: Reeves (2010).

improvement in implementation, the research shows that the greatest gains come from deep implementation and that there is a negligible difference between low and moderate levels of implementation.[4] In fact, in some cases, moderate implementation had a worse effect on achievement than no implementation at all (Figure 1.1).

This research should send a loud and clear message to teachers who work with ELLs that not only do we need to ensure that we are using the most effective strategies but that we need to be deeply implementing those strategies. Even more important, we need to be differentiating those strategies to meet the very diverse needs of the students we are working with.

Is It Only About Degree of Implementation?

English language learners have very specific needs, and those needs change depending on several factors, including:

- Proficiency in the primary language. A student's proficiency level in his or her primary language has been shown to be a predictor of success in acquiring a second language. A child who arrives in our schools with a solid foundation and a high level of proficiency and literacy in his or her native language will have a leg up on learning English.[5]

- Stability. A student's language acquisition is negatively affected if he or she has a high rate of transiency during his or her educational career.

- Maintenance of the native language. Students who maintain their native language are likely to outperform their English-only peers.[6]

- If the ELL has had previous educational experience, then success in our school system is only a matter of acclimation because his or her previously learned skills can be transferred to the new environment.

Factors such as these greatly impact the learning needs of the individual ELL. These examples illustrate why working with ELLs requires not only that we deeply implement high impact strategies, but also that we appropriately differentiate those strategies based on the very specific needs of each ELL. In Chapter Ten we will see firsthand the difference that differentiation makes for ELLs.

How Long It Takes to Acquire English

This is perhaps the most frequently asked question regarding ELLs, and there is no easy way to answer it. Like everything else surrounding the teaching of ELLs, the answer is complicated. The rate at which a child acquires a second language is dependent on several factors, with the most influential one being the amount of formal schooling the child had in his or her primary language. The most comprehensive study we have is a longitudinal study conducted by Wayne Thomas and Virginia Collier from 1982 to 1996.[7] In that study Thomas and Collier looked at the language acquisition of 700,000 students. They considered factors ranging from socioeconomic status to number of years of primary language schooling. Of all the factors considered, the amount of formal schooling prior to arriving in U.S. schools outweighed all other variables. Other findings from their studies include the following:

- Students between the ages of eight and eleven who had two to three years of formal schooling in their native language took five to seven years to test at grade level in English.

- Conversely, students with little or no formal schooling in their native language who arrived before the age of eight took seven to ten years to test at grade level in English.

- Students who were below grade level in their native language also took between seven and ten years to reach just the fiftieth percentile, and many of them never reached grade-level proficiency.

Cummins's research found that a significant level of fluency in conversational language can be achieved in two to three years. However, academic language required between five and seven years to reach near native proficiency levels.[8]

The number of immigrant, migrant, and refugee students in the United States who have limited English proficiency is growing exponentially. In fact, students who are learning English as a second language are the fastest-growing segment of the school-age population. Although the number of ELLs nationwide has skyrocketed, their academic achievement lags far behind that of their native English-speaking peers.

The New Wave of Immigration

The populations of elementary and secondary schools across the United States continue to change as a result of record high numbers of immigrants entering the country. Between 1970 and 2000, the number of school-age children of immigrants grew from 6 to 19 percent. The 1990s saw the number of children of immigrants grow more than 72 percent in secondary schools and 39 percent in elementary schools. This is particularly significant because many secondary schools are not yet structured to promote language acquisition and content-area mastery designed specifically for newcomers.[9]

A Growing ELL Population

Along with a growing number of immigrants, the population of ELLs has also grown dramatically. Between 1993 and 2003, the ELL population grew by 84 percent as the overall student population rose 12 percent. The number of ELLs in elementary schools from 1980 to 2000 increased from 5 to 7 percent, while in secondary schools, the number increased from 3 to 5 percent.

Populations of immigrants have increased for states with traditionally high numbers of ELLs as well as in other states. The following states experienced the largest increases:

Nevada: 206 percent

North Carolina: 153 percent

Georgia: 148 percent

Nebraska: 125 percent

These shifts have especially affected the large urban centers in these states that have become gateway cities, such as Las Vegas, Nevada; Charlotte, North Carolina; Atlanta, Georgia; and Omaha, Nebraska. The data show that ELLs are highly concentrated in a few urban schools that are also highly minority, low income, and disproportionately likely to fail federal standards.[10] In areas that are newly experiencing an influx of ELLs, the burden is often overwhelming because they often lack the resources and properly credentialed teachers to meet the needs of so many students. Such demographic trends have led to a crisis in educating ELLs.

Characteristics of the Current ELL Population

After English, Spanish is the most widely used language currently spoken in the United States. While it is estimated that approximately 20 percent of the school-age population speaks a language other than English, 14 to 16 percent of those children speak Spanish as their primary language at home.[11] The remaining 4 to 6 percent of these children speak a language other than Spanish. When we consider the K–5 population of ELLs, we find that the majority, 76 percent, speak Spanish and are of Latino/Hispanic background.[12]

The statistics for children who are about to enter our school system are important. The Early Childhood Longitudinal Study of Kindergarten Children, a national study that looked at more than twenty-two thousand students who were about to enter kindergarten in 1998, found that 68 percent of the children were classified as native English speakers, while 18 percent were classified as language minority (LM).[13] About 13 percent of the total sample were classified as Spanish speaking, 2.7 percent were identified as Asian speaking, and 2 percent spoke a European language. The majority of these language-minority students (52 percent) lived in high levels of poverty; strikingly, 80 percent of the Spanish speakers who were initially identified as being the least fluent in English were in the lowest two socioeconomic status quintiles. These data not only point to an increasingly diverse population, but also clearly show that many incoming language-minority students, particularly Hispanic, live in impoverished homes. These facts have clear implications for schools. We will see later in this book that the school becomes a lifeline for many of these students and their families, often offering resources that they would be unlikely to access otherwise. They reinforce the importance of connecting with these families on a much higher level than we may be accustomed to.

While most families in the United States consider school a place where children go to experience learning, for families living in poverty, school becomes a caretaker that provides their children such necessities as meals and health screenings in addition to an education.

Having taught in an urban setting with high levels of language-minority and low-socioeconomic status students, I saw firsthand the effect that poverty had on instruction. I often had students who had not eaten since having had lunch at school the previous day. Other than the obvious impact, these often desperate situations also brought to light the intense and often painful distractions that many of my students were dealing with while trying to learn. When even the most basic of needs are not being met, students face tremendous challenges to reaching academic and language proficiency.

Chapter 2

The Case for Urgency

In This Chapter

- No Child Left Behind (NCLB) legislation and its impact on the classroom

- Annual measurable achievement objectives defined

- The growing segregation of English learners

While demographic changes have presented states and districts that have not historically had high ELL populations with some daunting obstacles, states that have traditionally had high levels of ELLs continue to face challenges of their own. Nationally three challenges point to an evolving crisis in the education of ELLs.

The Impact of the No Child Left Behind Act

The first of these challenges comes indirectly from the implementation of legislation aimed at improving the education of all students. Within the No Child Left Behind Act of 2002, Title I and Title III contain provisions that specifically address ELLs. Title I requires schools to improve the performance of ELLs on assessments in reading and math. It also establishes that ELLs are a protected subgroup, along with other racial and ethnic groups, and requires schools to report their assessment results. Schools that do not meet the performance targets face restructuring or possible school closure.

Title III requires schools to measure and improve ELLs' language proficiency. It also holds states accountable for the improvement in language proficiency of ELLs on an annual basis and provides support for states and school districts to create new assessments of language proficiency.[1] Title III establishes three annual measurable achievement objectives (AMAOs) that all teachers need to be aware of:

AMAO 1: Establishes annual increases in the number or percentage of children making progress in learning English

AMAO 2: Establishes annual increases in the number or percentage of children attaining English language proficiency (reclassification) by the end of each school year

AMAO 3: Establishes adequate yearly progress for ELLs in meeting grade-level academic achievement standards in English language arts and mathematics

Because mainstream teachers in particular may not be familiar with AMAOs or with the growth targets that ELLs are expected to meet, the first order of business for the school is to make sure that all teachers know what the AMAOs mean to their instruction. The Resources section at the end of Part One provides a starting point for this to happen.

The challenge to educators lies in the unexpected impact that these provisions in NCLB have had on the landscape of teaching ELLs. Due to the increased focus on rapid acquisition of English, many more states, led by California, are placing ELLs in English immersion or mainstream classes.

Studies by Thomas and Collier have confirmed that efforts at rapid acquisition of a new language have detrimental effects on the long-term success of ELLs.[2] While students in English immersion classes may acquire language and reclassify more quickly, those gains quickly disappear when they reach middle and high school and the cognitive demands of school increase dramatically. At this point, these students have long been reclassified and are no longer receiving language support in the form of English as a Second Language (ESL) or English language development (ELD). Graduation becomes an unreachable goal, and many students end up dropping out. High ELL dropout rates create additional challenges for schools with high concentrations of second-language learners who must meet graduation standards required under NCLB for ELLs and other students. In Part Two, we conduct an audit of ELL programs and address questions regarding the efficacy of programs.

A second challenge appears in the bleak picture for ELLs painted by data from the 2000 Census. It revealed that most ELLs attending elementary and secondary schools were born and raised in the United States. In fact, over 75 percent of ELLs in elementary schools and over 50 percent of ELLs in secondary schools were born in the United States, and many of those students also had U.S.-born parents.[3] This leads us to conclude that U.S. schools have not served these students well. After seven or more years, these students have failed to become proficient in English. In fact, this group of students has led to yet another acronym, LTELs (long-term English learners). LTELs are students who for a variety of reasons, which we examine in Chapter Three, never reach proficiency in English.

The third major challenge that has emerged from census data is the growing segregation of ELLs. We know from demographic data that six states have high concentrations of school-age children of immigrants: California, New York, Texas, Florida, Illinois, and New Jersey. Fix and Capps have noted that in California, almost 50 percent of all school-age children were children of immigrants.[4]

State Concentrations of School-Age Children of Immigrants

This pattern of growing segregation of children of immigrants is also evident in states with relatively small but rapidly growing immigrant populations. These trends indicate that ELLs are not just attending schools that are economically and ethnically segregated, but also schools that are linguistically isolated.

Another disturbing trend is that these schools are disproportionately failing to meet state standards, and many are facing sanctions. ELLs are highly concentrated in the same schools in part because of residential segregation by race, ethnicity, and income. In 1999, over 53 percent of ELLs attended schools where more than 30 percent of all students were ELLs.[5]

Research from the Urban Institute has examined these schools with high ELL concentrations and found that they are typically larger than schools with few or no ELL students and have less experienced principals and teaching staffs.[6] A study by the American Education Research Association showing the educational and community benefits of integrated schools for both white and minority students confirmed that segregated, predominantly minority schools offer profoundly unequal educational opportunities.[7]

The children who attend predominantly minority schools experience this inequality in several ways: they have less qualified and less experienced teachers, high levels of instability caused by rapid turnover of teachers, fewer educational resources, and limited exposure to peers who can serve as role models and have a positive influence on their academic learning. These inequalities thus typically result in educational outcomes such as lower high school graduation rates and scores on standardized tests that are lower in schools with high percentages of white students.[8]

When nearly two-thirds of African American and Latino students attend schools where most students are eligible for free and reduced lunch, the sense of urgency for change becomes overwhelming.

According to Cleveland, a genuine crisis exists for Hispanic, African American, and economically deprived youth in urban areas. As recent demographic studies have shown, ELLs commonly fall into two of those categories: Hispanic and economically deprived.[9]

Responding to the Challenges

Thomas Jefferson wrote, "Whenever you do a thing, act as if all the world were watching." While most people read that quote and feel inspired to pretend that they are being watched, educators do not have that luxury; the fact is that everyone is watching.

As educators, we teach, and that act of teaching should have a positive result: learning for all. Unfortunately that end is not always attained. In fact, a staggering number of students drop out of school every year. Many drop out as a final act of desperation and hopelessness when faced with difficult challenges that they may believe cannot be solved by staying in school. For many of these students, their investment in learning has not paid off.

From parents to community members, policymakers to governmental officials, everyone has an opinion about how to improve teaching and learning. We are surrounded by opinions and ideas for what works. Because everyone has walked the halls of schools and spent considerable time within its walls, most people believe that they have intimate knowledge about the educational system that makes them expert on how to improve it.

While we are all eager to hear new ideas and learn better ways of doing things, we also need practical solutions grounded in research. Opinions, instincts, and intentions cannot guide critical decisions about teaching and learning.

In the past decade, we have been inundated by new initiatives, each claiming to be the solution we have been desperately waiting for. In fact, I would venture to say that it is precisely this eagerness to jump from one initiative to another that has often proven to be our worst enemy. Schools and, more important, teachers are feeling more fractured and overburdened than ever before because the intense pressure to show results has led them on a wild goose chase for the ultimate silver bullet. More often than not, what has been offered turns out to be a combination of disjointed programs and initiatives.

When an initiative fails to deliver, we drop it and move to the next one. It is for this reason that we need a call to sanity, a time-out, an opportunity to regroup and get back to what matters: ensuring the success of all students. We need to get back to the basics and remind ourselves what good instruction looks like.

Good-quality instruction for ELLs is a particular challenge. In spite of the overabundance of opinions on effective teaching strategies for ELLs, very little is backed by reliable research. In fact, as far back as 1997, Diane August and Kenji Hakuta showed how little actionable research there has been on teaching content to ELLs.[10] Although the research base has slightly increased since then, there is still much work to be done in the area of researching effective teaching strategies for English language learners. Until that body of research emerges, we face these challenges armed with existing research and knowledge of what works.

Chapter 3

Long-Term English Language Learners

In This Chapter

- Defining long-term English learners (LTELs)

- The factors that contribute to students becoming LTELs

- How to identify LTELs and provide them with the instruction they need to be reclassified for mainstream classes

Statistics show that the majority of secondary ELLs are long-term English learners (LTELs), defined as English learners who have been in U.S. schools for more than six years without reaching sufficient English proficiency to be reclassified for mainstream classes.[1] They are increasing in numbers, especially in states like California that have historically had high populations of ELLs. Most likely caused in California by the passage of legislation that largely eradicated state bilingual programs, it has now spread to other states largely because of the passage of similar legislation.[2]

Many states across the country are attempting to address the challenge of secondary English learners who have been in U.S. schools for as many as ten years without reaching proficiency in English. The disturbing fact that 56 percent of secondary ELLs were born in the United States points to the fact that schools have not effectively met the needs of this growing population. Although there is not yet a common definition for LTELs, the following statistics on cities and states reporting data for LTELs in secondary schools demonstrate the urgency of this issue:[3]

City or State	Percentage of Secondary Students Identified as LTEL
Dallas, Texas	70 percent
California	59 percent
New York, New York	33 percent
Colorado	23 percent

Although little research has been done with respect to LTELs, Olsen has discovered some common characteristics:[4]

- Seventy-five percent spent at least two years in a mainstream program with no ESL support.

- Twelve percent spent their entire schooling in mainstream classes and received no ESL support.

- Few LTELs received primary language instruction.

- Most LTELs were provided with curriculum and materials that did not meet the needs of ELLs.

- A majority were enrolled in weak English language development programs.

- These students have a history of inconsistent programs. For example, they may have been in a bilingual program in kindergarten and first grade, an English mainstream program in second grade, and a bilingual program in third grade.

- They experienced a narrowed curriculum focused on increased time in English language arts and math, with little or no time for science or social studies.

- They live and attend school in socially segregated and linguistically isolated areas.

- They have moved around a lot, both transnational moves and in and out of the United States for periods throughout their schooling.

It appears from the research that due to the growing numbers of ELLs facing many of these same conditions, there will be increasing numbers of LTELs in secondary classrooms. Without appropriate English language programs coupled with the support of a well-structured ESL program, LTELs face the possibility of becoming a statistic.

The first step toward ensuring that these students receive high-quality instruction is identifying them through assessment data. LTELs typically have low scores on state standardized tests and are most likely at level 3, speech emergence, in overall language acquisition. In fact, many of these students have become stuck at level 3 for many years. While they may sound proficient because of their broad social vocabulary, they lack the academic vocabulary to succeed in secondary core content classes. One dismal statistic that has emerged from examining the characteristics of LTELs in New York City schools found that the average grade for this group of students was 69.20 percent.[5] This type of feedback begins to slowly wear away at a student's motivation and desire to learn.

The Part One Resources section contains some ideas and strategies for filling gaps for LTELs. Chapter Twenty-Three presents strategies that can be used with all levels of ELLs that help them access content.

Chapter 4

How Children Acquire Language

In This Chapter

- Simultaneous versus sequential language acquisition
- The developmental stages of language acquisition
- Language mixing and code switching

Although language acquisition follows a predictable pattern of stages, what is not predictable is the amount of time that each of those stages may take. Much research has been done to try to identify the conditions or characteristics that influence the rate of acquisition, and what has become clear is that the speed of language acquisition stems from factors that are both within the child and in the child's learning environment. Specifically, the child's aptitude for languages, interest and motivation, and personality interact with the quantity and quality of language inputs and opportunities for use to influence the rate of language acquisition and eventual fluency levels.[1]

McLaughlin has distinguished simultaneous and sequential acquisition of language.[2] *Simultaneous acquisition* can be seen in young children, typically before the age of three, who seem to follow similar developmental pathways to learning a second language, as do children who learn just one language. Clearly this facility is why the majority of young children in the world who acquire two or more languages do so within the first few years of life.[3] The implication is that the exposure of children to learning multiple languages should happen as early in life as possible.

After the first three years of life, children who acquire a second language do so sequentially. They follow a different progression and pathway from that followed by monolingual children, and the progression is highly affected by the characteristics of the language learner as well as the characteristics of the language learning environment. By the time these children begin learning the second language, they have already learned the basics of their first language. They are familiar with and understand the structure of their primary language and must now learn the vocabulary, grammar, and syntax that are unique to the second language. The majority of the debate among linguists and researchers is driven by their beliefs of how best to teach these structures. Although we will not go deeply into these debates, we will explore different strategies that have at their core some of these beliefs.

Tabors and Snow have posited that sequential second-language acquisition is a developmental sequence that follows four distinct stages (these should not to be confused with language acquisition levels):[4]

1. *The home language stage.* The child holds on to the primary language, insisting instead that others learn to understand him or her. When ELLs who have become competent in their first language are put into an English-dominant setting such as a mainstream classroom, they continue to speak in their home language to other children even when these others do not understand them. Although this first stage typically lasts only a few days to a few weeks, sometimes a child continues in this stage for months.

2. *Nonverbal period.* Children realize that they cannot communicate in this setting using their home language. They move into a silent period and rarely speak, perhaps using nonverbal means to communicate. Although it may seem that little is happening, this is actually an active language learning stage for ELLs. They are listening in great detail and learning the features, sounds, and words of the second language, although they are not using it to communicate. Again, depending on the child, this stage may be very brief (days to weeks) or can last for months. This is an extremely important stage in the progression of learning a second language. Although second language learners may need to be assessed, any scores gathered at this time may underestimate a child's true language proficiency and thus result in misleading information.

3. *Telegraphic and formulaic speech.* The second language learner begins to produce predictable language. *Telegraphic* refers to the use of very simple phrases, often only two words, such as "Want eat," indicating that the child would like something to

eat. This is similar to the type of language structure that monolingual children experience when they are in the initial stages of language production. *Formulaic speech* refers to syllables of words strung together or a combined chunk of words that reflect words the child has heard. Tabors provides an example from one of the preschools she studied in which children used the phrase "Lookit" to get other students' attention or to get them to play.[5] ELLs develop these phrases in an attempt to help them achieve social goals.

4. *Productive language.* Students begin to create their own phrases that reflect their thoughts and desires. At the start of this stage, they may use a very simple pattern of noun, verb, noun; for example, "I need pencil." Their use of language becomes more sophisticated over time as they gain control over the structure, patterns, and vocabulary of the new language. Overt corrections should not be made, just as they wouldn't be made for a monolingual child learning to speak. Repetition of the correct phrase provides models of the language that they can mimic: "You need a pencil. Okay, here you go."

Language acquisition is a developmental process, and thus these stages are flexible and not mutually exclusive. McLaughlin, Blanchard, and Osanai accurately portrayed the process as acting more like the actions of waves, "moving in and out, generally moving in one direction, but receding, then moving forward again."[6]

Often ELLs mix languages (known as *language mixing*) or switch back and forth between words (known as *code switching*) in the two languages. Parents and teachers alike may be concerned that this is evidence of confusion on the child's part. In fact, this is a natural part of learning a second language. A student who is trying to relay a message or make known her needs may find that she lacks sufficient vocabulary. In an effort to communicate her message, she may rely on vocabulary from her native language that she may not yet be familiar with in the second language. Research has confirmed that language mixing is present even among adult bilinguals as they try to make a special emphasis or establish their cultural identity.[7]

These demographic trends point to the great diversity within the ELL population. English language learners vary in the home language they speak, the age at which they arrived in the United States, the age at which they were first exposed to English, their fluency rates in both their primary language and English, their years of schooling in their native country, and their family's socioeconomic status. What all of these variances point to is that there is no one-size-fits-all response to addressing the many needs of this increasingly diverse population. Instead, we must first clearly and accurately define our population and the characteristics that make them unique. Armed with that information, we are much better prepared to address their educational challenges.

Part One Resources

What Works with Long-Term English Learners

- *Urgency, acceleration, and focus.* LTELs are out of time. Many of them should be graduating from high school in a few years but won't because of their deficits. Their program requires focus and the use of high-impact strategies that can accelerate their learning.[1]

- *LTELs have distinct needs that have to be addressed.* Not all ELLs or LTELs have the same needs or require the same interventions. Each student needs a program designed specifically with his or her deficits and areas of strength in mind.

- *Language development is more than literacy development; LTELs need both.* LTELs require development in listening, speaking, reading, and writing rather than just literacy programs focused on reading skills. They need balance.

- *LTELs have both language development and academic gaps that must be addressed across the curriculum.* The entire school community has to work together to ensure that these students are receiving language development through content-area instruction, in addition to well-defined and separate ESL instruction that focuses solely on the structure and patterns of the English language.

- *Remember the crucial role of primary language development.* Many LTELs are not proficient in either their first or their second language, which greatly hampers their academic progress. Since so much of their English language development is built on knowledge in their primary language, we must ensure that LTELs receive specialized instruction in their first language that has been designed specifically for them.

- *LTELs need rigor.* There is no place for watered-down curriculum in the instructional plan for these students. They require challenging, relevant curriculum and assessments that build their confidence and help them see themselves as capable learners. (See Chapter Seven.)

- *LTELs need invitation, support, and insistence that they become active participants in their own education.* For too long, many of these students have been allowed to be invisible and take a passive role in their education. Teachers need to involve them in the process of getting them to reach proficiency. This can begin by having students keep track of their own data from common formative pre- and posttests. Witnessing their own progress from pre-to posttest, minimal as it may be, begins to challenge their beliefs about themselves as learners. Many of these students hope to attend college yet lack the skills to succeed in an academic program. We need to put them on a path to college graduation and help build their skills so that they can succeed. Work to build leadership abilities within them.

- *Relationships matter.* LTELs face daunting challenges. No one should face those challenges alone. They yearn for and need adult role models and mentors who care deeply about them and their success. Develop an LTEL mentor program.

- *LTELs need maximum integration with other students without sacrificing access to essential instruction.* We need to help LTELs break out of their isolated social bubbles and become integrated in the greater school community.

Discussion Questions

1. How has our school's English learner population changed over the past few years?

2. How has our teaching staff responded to these demographic changes?

3. How can we adjust to the changing demographics in order to best meet the needs of all students?

4. Do we have a population of LTELs? Can we identify the factors that are contributing to this growing population?

5. What initiatives have we adopted? Are those initiatives resulting in higher achievement for our students?

6. Do we need to take stock of our current state of instruction for English learners? If degree of implementation matters, how deeply are we implementing high-impact strategies?

7. Is our population of English learners highly segregated? How can we better respond to the needs of this isolated population?

Part Two

Getting Ready to Teach

The chapters in Part Two examine the initial identification of English learners, along with possible issues that may arise from an imperfect process. The chapters also explore English learner program options and challenge schools and districts to develop and implement program options that best meet the needs of the populations they serve.

Chapter 5

English Language Learner Instructional Programs

In This Chapter

- How to identify and place English learners

- Some issues to be aware of with home language surveys

- English learner program options

- Support programs for English learners

English language learners are initially identified based on their responses on the Home Language Survey. The Home Language Survey is administered when students register in school and is used to identify those who need to be assessed for language proficiency. Information provided by parents indicating that the child speaks a language other than English at home sets into motion a series of actions on the part of the school or district. At that point, a child is labeled a language-minority student. The next step is to determine whether the child qualifies for English learner status and, if so, the level of language proficiency for that child. (See Figure 7.1 in Chapter Seven.) If on the initial administration of the language proficiency assessment the child is deemed to be fluent, he or she is labeled fluent English proficient and does not qualify for ESL or bilingual services.

Some Issues with the Home Language Survey

Jamal Abedi, a professor at the University of California, Davis, School of Education, has raised concerns about the validity of using results from the Home Language Survey to place responses that parents provide to the Home Language Survey. His research has found that parents may provide inconsistent information for a variety of reasons, including concerns that their children will not receive an equitable education, fear or concerns over citizenship issues, or a general misunderstanding of the questions on the survey.[1]

Sometimes a parent may not accurately complete the Home Language Survey, which presents the school with a challenge. If the parent, for whatever reason, has responded in the negative to the questions on the Home Language Survey, the student may be mistakenly labeled as not needing an ESL program. In this situation, the student may need the support of an ESL program regardless of the fact he or she has not been officially labeled an ELL. The question that should always guide a school's instructional approach is, What does this student require to be successful? Ultimately it is the school's responsibility to provide whatever support a child needs in order to become proficient in English and achieve academically.

The best way to prevent this situation is to reassure parents that their child will not be stigmatized or receive any less of a quality education than English-only students. In past years, many communities have not viewed bilingual and English-immersion classrooms positively. Again, it is our responsibility to inform and educate parents and to ensure that we are offering high-quality educational programs that they can feel confident about placing their children in. Here are some recommendations:

- Ensure that the school's program offerings are the best possible options given the resources available to it.

- Ensure that program offerings are reflective of community demographics.

- Educate teachers and staff about the program offerings for ELLs. Often parents turn to teachers rather than to administrative personnel to ask questions, particularly if they already have a child in the school system.

- Provide information meetings, flyers, Web site articles, and other materials that communicate the options, as well as how those options were decided on. Parents want to know that the goal of their child's school is doing what's best for their child.

- Clearly explain the questions on the Home Language Survey to parents so that you are certain that they clearly understand them.

Home language surveys are developed by individual states and may even differ slightly in wording from district to district. This lack of consistency prompted Abedi to raise concerns about the validity of the survey.[2] If parents have had prior experiences enrolling their students in other states or districts, the inconsistency in language used on the home language surveys could result in inaccurate responses that could have a devastating effect on the student. This adds to the importance of ensuring clarity for parents regarding the completion of informational surveys. Short and Fitzsimmons share these concerns and make some recommendations of their own.[3] Because of the wide diversity within a single school's population of English learners, they recommend revising the Home Language Survey to ensure that parents are providing relevant information regarding their children on these topics:

- Native language skills

- Immigration generation

- The child's age on enrollment in U.S. schools

- A mobility history, which includes the number of times the student has left the country, for how long each time, whether the student attended school in his or native country, and whether the student was enrolled back in U.S. schools between visits

This type of information, when coupled with high-quality language proficiency assessments, ensures that students will be placed appropriately.

English Language Learner Program Options

Once a child has been officially identified as an English language learner (ELL) or limited English proficient (LEP), he will be placed in a program based on his needs and, more significant, the school's resources and offerings.

There is no single program for ELLs that is right for all students. The demographic profile of our nation is changing, and the same demographic changes are not being experienced everywhere equally. Every time I am asked, "What programs work best for ELLs?" I feel a certain sense of frustration. I can certainly share programs and strategies that are research based and have been shown to have a positive impact on student achievement, but the school and community must work together to implement them in a way that works best for the specific needs of their student population.

ELLs differ in their educational backgrounds, social experiences, cultural norms, and knowledge of English. All of these factors have their own impact on each individual student and should therefore influence the program offerings and implementation of the strategies schools use. Although bodies of long-term research such as that by Thomas and Collier have found that bilingual and dual-immersion programs have the best long-term impact on ELL achievement, not all schools and districts have the resources to implement these programs fully and effectively.[4] In that case, it would be counterproductive to attempt to implement a less-than-effective bilingual program, which may end up having a negative impact on achievement for a school's ELLs. The sections that follow explore some ELL program options.

Bilingual Programs

A bilingual program develops primary language (L1) literacy while also teaching English. There are two models of bilingual programs: *early exit*, in which ELLs are quickly transitioned into all-English instruction, and *late exit*, in which students are kept in the home language as long as possible and are gradually transitioned into all-English instruction. Late exit programs show much greater success.[5] The core subjects such as language arts, math, social studies, and science are taught in the primary language. Then depending on the type of program, English is introduced at varying rates. In addition, all students have a structured ESL program that supports the teaching of the form and function of the English language. Typically when students reach cognitive proficiency in their primary language as well as intermediate fluency in English, they are gradually transitioned into English for the core subjects.

When the following conditions are met, the bilingual program is perhaps one of the best options available for ELLs:

- The school has a cohesive, well-organized bilingual program and can offer it to the student for as long as possible, at least through fifth or sixth grade.[6]

- Students are provided a minimum thirty minutes daily of high-quality ESL instruction.

- The school is able to provide a highly qualified, fully credentialed, bilingual teacher for each grade level through at least fifth or sixth grade.

Dual-Immersion Programs

In this type of program, also referred to as bilingual immersion, dual language, developmental bilingual education, or two-way immersion, every student is immersed in learning to speak two languages simultaneously. In other words, ELLs are maintaining their primary language while learning English, and English-only students are learning a second language while learning their regular content. The method for achieving this differs greatly, with some schools opting for the fifty-fifty split, with English accounting for 50 percent of the day and the second language (L2) accounting for the remaining 50 percent. Regardless of the model used, the goal in this program is for all students to leave the school being bilingual. Research has shown that along with the bilingual program, this is one of the most effective of all ELL program options.[7]

English-Immersion Programs

In this program, students receive a percentage of instruction in their primary language and a percentage in English. Typically the minimum rate of L1 to L2 is a fifty-fifty split. Teachers in English-immersion classrooms use primary language and sheltered instructional strategies, which help make the content comprehensible, to help ELLs fully access the content. Successful implementation of English immersion is dependent on the same conditions for bilingual programs being met. English immersion is an effective program for ELLs.

English Mainstream

Although this is not considered an ELL program because it provides no primary language support, currently California, Arizona, and Massachusetts place the majority of their ELLs in mainstream classes.[8] English mainstream programs place students in an English-only classroom and provide limited resources for their first language. This is often referred to as a sink-or-swim program. Long-term studies have found that while initially students in English-only programs are reclassified surprisingly quickly and do quite well in early elementary school, their long-term achievement is not so positive. Once these students reach middle school and high school, they begin to lose much of the ground they had gained initially. Ultimately they are not able to sustain the gains they made during elementary school and struggle tremendously to keep up with their English-only peers.[9] For example, if students have not developed sufficient academic language, they will not fully understand their textbooks in middle and high school. For obvious reasons, English immersion programs are not the best option for all ELLs.

Support Programs for ELLs

In addition to determining the best program options for ELLs, we must also ensure there are appropriate support programs to meet their needs. These support programs include instruction in the structure and patterns of the English language, as well as strategies used to make the content accessible to students at all levels of language acquisition.

English as a Second Language Instruction

English language learners, regardless of whether they are in a bilingual, immersion, or mainstream program, should receive a minimal amount of ESL instruction. This instruction focuses on teaching the structures and patterns of the English language and may be offered as either a pull-out program, in which students are pulled out of the regular classroom to receive daily ESL instruction, or a push-in program, in which the ESL teacher comes into the regular classroom to provide ESL instruction within the context of the regular school day.

Sheltered Instruction

Sheltered instruction refers to a set of strategies used to teach core content to ELLs. These strategies help students access content despite their limited proficiency in English. ELLs at the intermediate fluency stage of language acquisition and above benefit the most from the use of these strategies.

Total Physical Response

Developed by James Asher in the 1970s, total physical response (TPR) is a set of strategies that help ELLs in the beginning levels of language acquisition access the content.[10] These strategies use commands, modeling, body movements, and gestures to establish communication in the very early stages of language acquisition. TPR is a specific set of strategies that need to be implemented with fidelity. It is not enough to add physical movements to lessons and call it TPR.

Conclusion

Program options for ELLs must be carefully planned and thought out. It is not enough to merely say that a school or district has a dual-immersion program. It must instead clearly define that program based on the resources available. It is not always feasible to offer programs such as bilingual if they cannot be fully implemented or implemented in a way that is educationally sound for a school's students. Considerations such as these need to be taken into account when developing English language programs or auditing current offerings. (See the Part Two Resources section for information on English language program offerings.)

Chapter 6

Levels of Language Acquisition

In This Chapter

- The importance of teachers' knowing and understanding language acquisition levels
- Descriptions of the levels of language acquisitions
- How the four language domains develop
- Basic descriptors of language acquisition levels
- Planning instruction
- High-level thinking for all English learners

Title III of the No Child Left Behind Act requires states to identify English language proficiency standards. Within these standards documents, states establish their own levels of language proficiency. In this chapter, I define levels of language acquisition. It is important to clearly distinguish between language proficiency levels and language acquisition levels. These two terms are often used interchangeably, but they are not the same. *Language proficiency* refers to an identifiable state of proficiency based on the results of a language proficiency assessment. In contrast, *language acquisition* levels refer to the research-based, predictable levels through which children progress on the way to proficiency in the target language. Linguists explain that language acquisition is a subconscious process similar to the way in which we acquired our first language. Thus, language acquisition levels describe the characteristics of a child as he or she progresses through a defined level of language acquisition.

School leaders should ensure that every educator who comes in contact with ELLs is aware of the different stages of language acquisition. Knowing and understanding these levels helps all teachers identify appropriate strategies to use with ELLs. ESL teachers may already have vast knowledge about language acquisition levels. Mainstream teachers who may encounter ELLs during their content-area instruction benefit greatly from understanding these levels as well. Table 6.1 provides a description of each language acquisition level.

How the Four Language Domains Develop in ELLs

Table 6.2 shows the five language acquisition levels and the language domains that are likely to dominate those levels. Notice that in the early levels of language acquisition, language production is mostly in the receptive domains of listening and reading. As ELLs' language acquisition increases, they begin to develop the productive domains of speaking and writing. A common misconception about language acquisition levels is that teachers should delay the most complex of the productive domains, writing, until the later levels of language proficiency. To help dispel this myth, Table 6.2 shows an accurate representation of how the domains develop. Notice that there is no point at which students should not be attempting to produce language. The table does, however, show that although all the domains should be activated at all acquisition levels, students will be more dependent on listening, especially at the early levels, and reading and writing will naturally develop more slowly than the other three domains.

Common Misconceptions

One common misconception is that because English learners are more dependent on the domain of listening in the beginning, they should not be given material that requires them to engage in the other domains of language whenever they feel ready to do so. In fact, English learners should have opportunities every day to engage in the four domains of language.

As you plan instruction for level 1 and 2 English learners, ensure that you are not excluding them from any of the other domains of language. Some effective strategies for encouraging and supporting English learners include using sentence starters in speaking and writing. In fact, classroom walls should be covered in language that students can use—for example, academic vocabulary, questioning prompts, and response prompts.

Table 6.1 Levels of Language Acquisition

Language Acquisition Level	Approximate Length of Time	Speaking and Writing Descriptors
Level 1: Pre-production	0 to 6 months	Speaks in single words May respond with two- or three-word phrases Has a very limited vocabulary (mostly basic interpersonal communication skills) Uses drawings to communicate thoughts and ideas Points or gestures to communicate basic needs Dependent on native language
Level 2: Early production	6 months to 1 year	Speaks in short phrases and fragments Begins to use short, simple sentences May point or gesture to communicate preferences (for example, in answer to "Do you want a hamburger or hot dog?") Has a limited but basic vocabulary consisting mostly of basic interpersonal communication skills Errors in grammar may hamper meaning Uses familiar words and phrases
Level 3: Speech emergence	1 to 3 years	Speaks using simple, uncomplicated sentences Begins to vary sentence structure Uses appropriate grammar and word order, but errors are still common Uses present or past tense only Errors may still hamper meaning Begins to use basic academic knowledge from content areas Emerging fluency
Level 4: Intermediate fluency	3 to 5 years	Uses complete sentences Uses varied sentence structure Uses a range of vocabulary sufficient to express ideas Uses appropriate word order and grammar but may make minor errors Begins to experiment with more complex verb forms Errors rarely interfere with communication Often must reread for meaning Uses academic vocabulary Use details when retelling or relating personal stories Improved narrative writing

(Continued)

Table 6.1 Levels of Language Acquisition (Continued)

Language Acquisition Level	Approximate Length of Time	Speaking and Writing Descriptors
Level 5: Advanced fluency	5 to 7 years	Writes complete sentences
		Writes narratives
		Uses complex verb forms
		Uses varied and complex sentence structure
		Has a broad social and academic vocabulary
		Uses grammar and word order approximating that of a native speaker
		Errors no longer interfere with communication
		Has grade-level-appropriate fluency approximating that of a native speaker
		Reads for meaning
		Correctly uses academic language

Source: Adapted from Krashen and Terrell (1983).

Table 6.2 When Language Domains Develop

Language Acquisition Levels	Listening	Speaking	Reading	Writing
Preproduction	D	L	L	L
Early production	D	L	L	L
Speech emergence	D	D	L	L
Intermediate fluency	D	D	L	D
Advanced fluency	D	D	D	D

Note: L = Limited use of this domain by the English learner. D = Dominant use of this domain by the English learner.

These are all valuable scaffolds for ELLs. Remember that the idea is to provide the support in the event that a student feels ready. One of the tenets of total physical response is that English learners should have the right to remain silent until they feel ready to move on.[1]

Another common misconception when working with English learners is that students at the beginning levels of language acquisition are not ready to use critical-thinking skills at the highest levels of Bloom's Taxonomy. The real challenge is not whether they are capable of doing it, but rather whether we can pose questions and provide opportunities for English learners at all levels to think critically.

Table 6.3 Differentiated Question Prompts by Level

	Knowledge	Comprehension	Application	Analysis	Synthesis	Evaluation
Level 1	Show Point List Which	Identify Recognize Illustrate	Sketch Construct Build	Diagram	Arrange Construct Assemble	Indicate Select
Level 2	Show Point List Which	Identify Recognize Illustrate Demonstrate	Sketch Construct Build Choose Demonstrate	Diagram Classify	Arrange Construct Assemble Collect	Indicate Select Choose
Level 3	Name Recall Tell	Tell Describe Rearrange Predict	Use Plan	Question Experiment Test Describe	Write Create Plan Prepare	Estimate Consider
Level 4	What When How	Compare Contrast	Dramatize Plan How	Relate Support Explain	Design Compose Propose	Judge Assess Value
Level 5	How	Compare Contrast Extend	Consider Test Apply	Analyze Compare Contrast Debate Examine	Formulate Suggest	Defend

Table 6.3 shows the levels of Bloom's Taxonomy along with the verbs we can use to formulate questions. The verbs have been grouped by level in order to facilitate their use with English learners at all levels.

Conclusion

Once we accurately identify an English learner's language proficiency level, instruction at the appropriate level is critical to the student's successful progression through the different levels of language acquisition. The progression of a student who does not receive appropriately leveled instruction will likely stall. Challenging English learners by using questioning prompts that match their level is one of several effective strategies to use.

Chapter 7

Assessing English Language Learners

In This Chapter

- Complexities in assessing English learners
- Determining the purpose for assessment
- Complexities in monitoring language acquisition
- Assessing language proficiency and content knowledge
- Developing differentiated assessments

One of the most complex issues surrounding English language learners lies in the question of how to accurately assess their progress. What lends to the complexity is the fact that there are so many different purposes for assessing these learners: classification, program placement, monitoring of academic progress, and reclassification, for example. Our first task, then, is to determine the purpose for assessment in order to design an assessment measure that matches our purpose and yields the information we are looking for.

Formative and Summative Assessments

The purpose for assessing academic progress can be formative or summative. *Formative assessments* take place while the learning is happening and thus provide valuable diagnostic information that guides the selection of instructional strategies and the instruction itself. Any assessment of language proficiency should be considered formative in nature since students are in the process of acquiring the English language for at least seven years. *Summative assessments* provide the final confirmation that a student has mastered the content and is ready to move to the next unit of study.[1]

Regardless of whether the assessment is formative or summative, the bottom line is that teachers from all content areas need to be able to determine what English learners know or don't know regardless of their language proficiency levels. This presents some obvious challenges, particularly for mainstream content teachers who may not know how to differentiate their assessments so that even an English learner at the beginning levels of language acquisition can demonstrate his or her understanding of the content.

In the early elementary grades and beginning levels of language acquisition, when many students lack reading and writing skills, teachers need to depend on performance-based assessments to be able to assess a student's understanding of a concept or skill accurately.

The Assessment Process

Clearly identifying the purpose of an assessment will help drive the type of assessment to use.

The first assessment of ELLs is conducted in order to determine initial classification and program placement. The diagram in Figure 7.1 outlines how this is accomplished.

Monitoring Language Acquisition

Once the student's initial language acquisition level has been identified, the ESL teacher is responsible for monitoring his or her language proficiency. Particularly in the early stages of language development, the student will rapidly progress through the initial stages of preproduction (up to six months) and early production (six months to one year). This rapid progression mostly involves social language, that is, basic interpersonal communication skills (BICS).

Complexities of Monitoring Language Acquisition

Many experts in the field of teaching English to English language learners have failed to shed light on one particular complexity: using the results of language proficiency assessments to plan instruction. Throughout the remainder of this book, I reinforce the importance of the use of this information, as well as the importance of sharing this with all teachers of English learners, because of its significance to the process of language development.

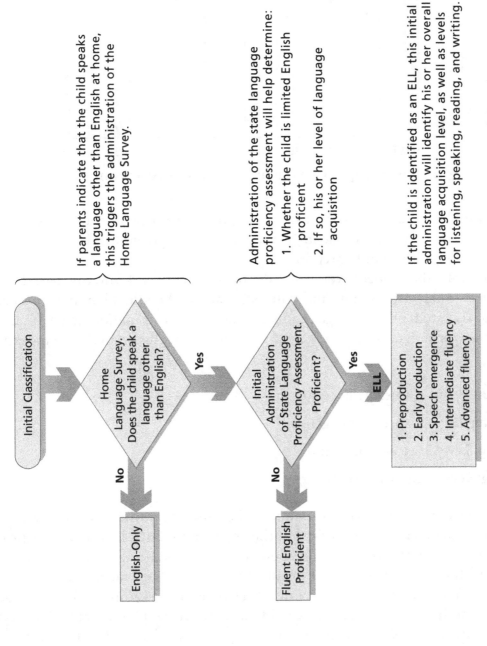

Initial Classification

If parents indicate that the child speaks a language other than English at home, this triggers the administration of the Home Language Survey.

Home Language Survey. Does the child speak a language other than English?

No → English-Only

Yes →

Initial Administration of State Language Proficiency Assessment. Proficient?

Administration of the state language proficiency assessment will help determine:

1. Whether the child is limited English proficient
2. If so, his or her level of language acquisition

No → Fluent English Proficient

Yes → **ELL**

1. Preproduction
2. Early production
3. Speech emergence
4. Intermediate fluency
5. Advanced fluency

If the child is identified as an ELL, this initial administration will identify his or her overall language acquisition level, as well as levels for listening, speaking, reading, and writing.

Figure 7.1 The Initial Classification and Program Placement

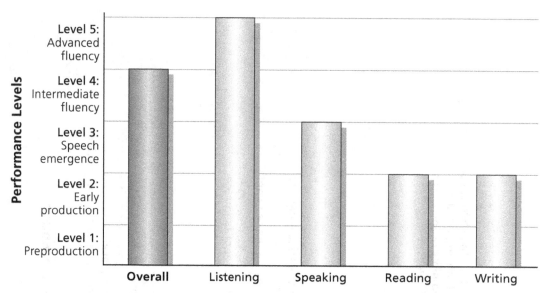

Figure 7.2 Sample Language Proficiency Assessment

After the initial administration of the language proficiency assessment, teachers should receive a report that identifies the student's overall level of language acquisition. Figure 7.2 provides an example of this kind of report.

In this example, the student would be identified as a level 4, intermediate fluency. Although this is vital information and will assist all teachers in planning instruction appropriate to this student's language acquisition level, the information listed for each of the four domains is perhaps of even greater importance. For this student, the breakdown is as follows:

- Listening: Level 5, intermediate fluency

- Speaking: Level 3, speech emergence

- Reading: Level 2, early production

- Writing: Level 2, intermediate fluency

The levels for each domain are so significant because the purpose of this assessment is to help guide placement of the student in the appropriate ESL class, as well as provide useful information for the regular education teachers. Not being aware of the scores for all domains for a particular student would greatly impede a teacher's ability to plan appropriately differentiated lessons for English learners. For example, a history teacher who assumes that this student is a level 4 would expect to see her perform at high levels and may not understand why she is struggling to comprehend the text. The knowledge that this student is a level 2 in reading would have been sufficient to understand that she might need to be provided with a low-readability text that would help her access the content. At a minimum, the teacher would understand that there is a valid reason as to why this student is struggling with the text.

Being uninformed about these levels may have led to several inaccurate assumptions about this student, including that the student is not engaged or that she has a learning disability since she is a level 4 but is unable to read and comprehend the textbook. Either of these assumptions could be detrimental to the success of any student, particularly ELLs. For that reason, all teachers, not just the ESL teacher, must know each student's language acquisition level for each domain in addition to the overall score.

Assessment in the ESL Classroom

According to Title III of the No Child Left Behind Act, states are required to conduct an annual standards-based assessment of English language proficiency for each ELL. This is the same assessment that is administered to determine an initial language acquisition level. While most schools use the results of this assessment to make an initial placement, they also use it to place students in the appropriate ESL classroom.

In addition to this annual assessment, ESL teachers should conduct their own progress monitoring of each ELL's language proficiency levels on an ongoing basis. Figure 7.3 illustrates the importance of progress monitoring for ELLs. The purpose of this assessment is to provide both ESL and mainstream classroom teachers with accurate information about a student's language proficiency levels so that they can plan appropriate instruction that will help the student reach the next level of language acquisition.

Questions to Consider

1. What impact does progress monitoring in the ESL class have on language acquisition?

2. What impact does progress monitoring in the ESL class have on mainstream teachers?

Assessment in the Mainstream Classroom

Often mainstream teachers feel out of the loop when it comes to educating ELLs. In fact, in the past, ESL teachers often failed to inform the mainstream teachers about the levels of their ELLs. As we have just seen, it is imperative that mainstream teachers be provided with language proficiency assessment data that includes overall levels as well as domain-specific levels for each English learner they teach. Some schools develop a student information

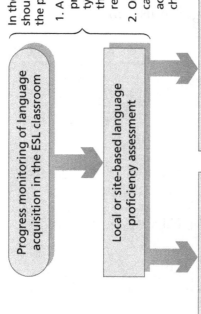

Progress monitoring of language acquisition in the ESL classroom

In the ESL classroom, language proficiency levels should be assessed at least once a trimester. What is the purpose of assessing them so often?

1. A common issue with state English language proficiency assessments is that results are not typically received in a timely manner. As a result, the scores are already outdated when the teacher receives them.

2. Our local English language proficiency assessment can help us determine if the student's language acquisition level in any of the four domains has changed.

Local or site-based language proficiency assessment

ESL Classroom

* A change in overall levels results in new placement in an appropriately leveled ESL class.

* Any change of English language acquisition level in individual domains helps the ESL teacher appropriately challenge ELLs based on their proficiency in each domain. For example, if the ELL level in writing changes from level 2 to level 3, the ESL teacher is able to modify written assignments to reflect the new level.

Mainstream Classroom

* Any change in English language acquisition level in individual domains helps the mainstream teacher appropriately challenge ELLs in the core content areas. If a student's language acquisition level in reading changes from level 3 to level 4, then the math, science, and history teachers can expect the ELL to access content from the textbook with less support and scaffolding, allowing the ELL to progress further in reading.

Key Term

Language Domains: The four language domains assessed annually by state English language proficiency assessments. In addition to an overall language acquisition level, students also receive a score in each of the four domains: listening, speaking, reading, and writing.

Figure 7.3 Progress Monitoring of Language Acquisition Levels

sheet that is updated periodically to reflect the most current information available on the language acquisition levels of English learners. The English Learner Profile Sheet, such as the example in the Part Two Resources section, should be filled out and distributed to all ESL and mainstream teachers.

In order for ELLs to make appropriate academic gains as well as gains in language acquisition, mainstream teachers need to provide appropriately leveled instruction and assessments.

Table 7.1 is an example of how English language acquisition levels can be used in conjunction with a state's English proficiency standards or World-Class Instructional Design and Assessment (WIDA) standards, to help plan appropriate performance-based assessments. (WIDA is a consortium of twenty-four partner states that developed a set of consistent language proficiency standards and assessments.) The results of these assessments can help mainstream teachers determine whether an ELL has mastered the content. It is especially significant to note in this example that the content has not been watered down from level 5 to level 1. Note in Table 7.1 that the science standard is listed at the top as a reminder of what it is that all students are expected to know and be able to do.

The differentiated assessment tasks reflect the WIDA writing and speaking descriptors for each level of language proficiency. If we look at the task for a level 1 student, we should feel confident that given the differentiation provided, the teacher would be able to determine whether this student is proficient on this science standard. Notice how level 1 students are expected to accomplish the same assessment task as the students in the other level; however, they are provided with scaffolds that allow them to demonstrate proficiency with limited English skills.

Planning Differentiated Assessments

Because ensuring learning for all students is the goal, we cannot afford not to differentiate assessments for English learners. There is no denying, however, that creating differentiated assessments is time intensive. Here are some ideas for easing some of the burden:

- Divide and conquer. Work with your colleagues, including the ESL teacher, and divide up the assessments. In this way, everyone will share the responsibility of creating the assessments, and there will be a year's worth of assessments written by the end of the year that can be used next year.

- Plan on developing two or three significant differentiated assessments that you will develop this year. Each year, you can develop two or three more. This approach will allow you the time to implement in a thoughtful manner.

Table 7.1 Using English Language Acquisition Levels to Plan Performance–Based Assessments

Standard: 7. Scientific progress is made by asking meaningful questions and conducting careful investigations. Substandard d: Communicate the steps and results from an investigation in written reports and verbal presentations.

Language Acquisition Level	Level 1: Preproduction	Level 2: Early Production	Level 3: Speech Emergence	Level 4: Intermediate Fluency	Level 5: Advanced Fluency
Differentiated tasks	1. Use word bank to complete data collection chart and lab. 2. Draw and then label lab steps and results using a word bank. 3. Share results with a partner.	1. Complete data collection chart and lab. 2. Draw and label lab steps and results using sentence starters. 3. Prepare and deliver a short presentation of findings. 4. Answer yes/no and WH (who, what, when, where) questions.	1. Complete data collection chart and lab. 2. Complete lab write-up using simple sentences. 3. Prepare and deliver a short presentation that narrates the steps in the lab and results.	1. Complete data collection chart and lab. 2. Complete lab write-up. 3. Present results and conclusions in a written report and orally.	1. Complete data collection chart and lab. 2. Complete lab write-up. 3. Communicate results and conclusions in a written report and verbal presentation.

Corresponding WIDA Level[a]	Level 1: Entering	Level 2: Beginning	Level 3: Developing	Level 4: Expanding	Level 5: Bridging
Selected WIDA Can Do writing descriptors for grades 6 to 8	• Draw content-related pictures. • Label pictures and graphs. • Generate lists from pretaught words/phrases and word banks.	• Extend "sentence starters" with original ideas. • Respond to yes/no, choice, and some WH questions.	• Explain steps in problem solving. • Give opinions, preferences, and reactions.	• Justify ideas. • Produce content-related reports. • Use details and examples to support ideas. • Take notes (for example, for research).	• Create expository text to explain graphs and charts. • Produce research reports using multiple sources and citations.
Selected WIDA Can Do speaking descriptors for grades 6 to 8	• Begin to use general and high-frequency vocabulary. • Answer select WH questions within the context of lessons or personal experiences.	• Convey content through high-frequency words and phrases. • State big or main ideas of classroom conversation.	• Give brief oral content-based presentations. • Connect ideas in discourse using transitions (for example, *but, then*).	• Paraphrase and summarize ideas presented orally. • Explain outcomes. • Explain and compare content-based concepts.	• Communicate with fluency in social and academic contexts. • Discuss and give examples of abstract, content-based ideas (such as democracy, justice).

[a] According to the WIDA Web site, the CAN DO descriptors provide a starting point for working with ELLs and are a collaborative tool for planning.

Questions to Consider

1. Is the content standard a power/essential standard? These are standards that meet the criteria of endurance (the standard is a life skill), leverage (a standard that is heavily assessed on standardized tests), and readiness for the next grade level (a standard that is important in school from this year on).[2] If so, this is a high-priority standard that all students need to master. Differentiation of the assessment tasks is essential.

2. How will my native English speakers demonstrate proficiency on this standard? How can I appropriately differentiate that task for my English language learners?

3. How can I use my state's English language proficiency standards to help me design similar tasks for the different levels? In most cases, these standards clearly define what students can do at each proficiency level and in each domain.

4. If your state does not have well-written ELP standards, then consider using other resources, such as WIDA standards or Can Do descriptors.

5. How can you use all four language domains in planning your tasks?

Although differentiation takes time, the cost of not doing it is enormous. It bears stating that without appropriate differentiation, assessment results will be inaccurate at best. Larry Ainsworth, senior professional development associate for the Leadership and Learning Center, writes that assessments help teachers make inferences about student achievement.[3] If the assessments are not well aligned, however, then it's fair to say that the inferences will be invalid. Here are some ideas that may help in developing differentiated assessments:

1. Familiarize yourself with your state's English language proficiency standards for your grade level. Keep in mind that most states have written these standards by grade span.

2. Plan differentiated tasks only for the levels of ELLs in your class. For example, if you have no level 1 or 2 students, then don't plan tasks for those levels.

Ideas

3. Keep the assessment tasks as similar as possible.

4. Notice that by level 5, ELL students should be conducting tasks that are similar to, or even the same tasks as, native English speakers.

And as you take on this task, bear in mind that planning differentiated tasks will become second nature eventually.

A Word of Caution to Mainstream Teachers

As a mainstream teacher, you may not be aware of all of the language acquisition levels of the ELLs in your classroom. This is not unusual. Material in the Part Two Resources section will help keep you informed about these levels.

In the meantime, there is an important caveat: typical ELLs develop basic interpersonal communication skills (BICS) in about one or two years, which means that you may not be able to distinguish who the ELLs are in your classroom just by listening to them. And it is possible that some ELLs in your room have reached level 3 (speech emergence) or even higher in the domain of speaking. Therefore, ELLs who have developed strong BICS and social vocabulary may sound proficient to you. You may assume, in fact, that these students comprehend classroom activities, your lectures, and the textbook when in fact they do not. Identifying a level for ELLs may not be easy. Keep in mind that while an individual ELL may be assigned an overall level, he or she may be at different levels of language acquisition in different domains.

Moreover, you may need to do your own informal assessment while you are waiting for official notification of levels. To do this, take some time to have an ELL read a passage aloud to you or silently, and then ask the student a few comprehension questions. If the student struggles, you know that this student's level in reading is at a lower level than his or her speaking.

Cognitive academic language proficiency (CALP) takes between five and seven years to develop. It may take longer depending on several factors, including the number of years that the child attended school in his or her native country. Students who arrive between the ages of eight and eleven and who attended school prior to arriving in the United States will not only acquire CALP at a faster rate, but will also progress through the levels of language acquisition at a faster rate. Students in your mainstream classroom who may have limited prior educational experience may take as long as seven to ten years to acquire CALP.

The Bottom Line

Get to know your students as much as possible, and use that information to help you plan appropriate instruction and assessments. You may also want to schedule some time to meet with the ESL teacher or ELL coordinator. Talk to your administrator about providing some time for ESL teachers and mainstream teachers to collaborate.

Chapter 8

Grading English Language Learners

In This Chapter

- Complexities in grading English learners
- The impact of an inaccurate grading system on students
- Resources for developing a grading policy for English learners

G rading is among one of the most controversial subjects in education. Research has shown that there are many reasons for this, but I believe that a main one is that it is one of the last areas in which teachers feel they have some semblance of control. Certainly we like to believe that grades are the one true objective measure of success or failure in the classroom, but there has been too much research to the contrary. Such experts in the field as Ken O'Connor and Douglas Reeves have made it quite clear that grades are anything but objective, much less true reflections of a student's success or failure.[1] Even in this era of standards, grades on those standards are often influenced by elements wholly unrelated to mastery of the standards. Issues about grading can be resolved only if we have clarity of purpose. Here are some questions that schools and districts need to grapple with when it comes to grading ELLs.

Questions to Consider

1. What purposes do grades serve?

   - Communication to parents?

   - Communication to students?

   - Communication to teachers?

2. If the purpose is communication, then does the school's grading policy allow teachers to communicate accurately the progress that ELLs are making in these areas:

   - Core content areas: Reading, math, history, science?

   - English language acquisition?

3. If the answer to question 2 is no, what first steps can we take to change that?

Impact of an Inaccurate Grading System on Students and Parents

Figure 8.1 reflects the type of grading report that ELLs often receive. These reports are often vague and do not provide clear and consistent information regarding the progress of ELLs. Look at this figure and consider what parents and students might learn from the grading policy reflected in this report. Then reflect on Questions to Consider.

Questions to Consider

1. Imagine that you are this student or this student's parent, and it is the end of the year. What exactly does this report card communicate to you?

How to Reach and Teach English Language Learners

2. Surely this student has made some academic progress over the course of the year. Are you able to tell from this report card how much progress this student has made?

3. What if you had received the same report for the past two years? How would you feel if you were the student? How motivated would you be to continue trying?

4. How would you feel if you were the parent? How would you feel as the teacher?

It is clear from the report card in Figure 8.1 that students are being graded according to progress toward English language arts (ELA) standards. The fact that this report does not show progress for ELLs is a problem. ELLs and their parents do not receive any usable information from this report. The student and parents are unable to see areas of strength or weakness and cannot determine what to do to improve performance in these areas. Certainly it is critical that parents see how their students are performing toward the ELA standards, but it is equally as critical for parents of ELLs and the students themselves to know how they are progressing in their acquisition of the English language. Parents and students also deserve to see progress and growth. In Questions to Consider, question 3 asked how motivated you would be to continue trying if you had received the same grades

Academic Achievement Key

4 = Exemplary	3 = Proficient	2 = Partially Proficient	1 = Not Proficient

	1st	2nd	3rd
Reading–Academic Achievement			
Decoding and Word Recognition			
1.1 Know and use complex word families when reading (e.g., -*ight*) to decode unfamiliar words	1	1	1
1.2 Decode regular multi-syllabic words	1	1	1
Vocabulary Development			
1.4 Use knowledge of antonyms, synonyms, homophones, and homographs	1	1	1
1.6 Use sentence and word context to find the meaning of unknown words	1	1	1
1.8 Use knowledge of prefixes and suffixes to determine the	1		

Figure 8.1 Profile for an ELL Level 2 Student

for three years. This is a critical question, particularly considering the dropout statistics for ELLs. According to some reports, some states are experiencing dropout rates as high as 50 percent for ELLs.[2] Achievement equals motivation, so when students do not see themselves as capable learners, the chances of their being engaged are slim. The motivation of adolescents to read and have high levels of engagement in their subject matter, Catherine Snow writes, depends on a number of factors. "Chief among these," she says, "is the adolescent's perception of how competent he or she is as a reader. It is the belief in the self (or lack of such belief) that makes a difference in how competent the individual feels."[3]

What About the Teacher's Beliefs?

We have seen how facing failing grades year after year can be detrimental to ELLs' development and attitudes toward learning. Now we will look at how failing grades affect teacher attitudes toward their students.

That past performance influences teachers' attitudes is well known. As much as we want to ignore the past performance of students and allow each of them the opportunity for a fresh start each school year, those comments, coupled with a student's defeatist attitude, may play out to be a self-fulfilling prophecy for both the student and the teacher. Students' past performance greatly influences teachers' perceptions and, worse, their expectations for what a student can achieve. In fact, Guskey postulates that "significant change in the beliefs and attitudes of teachers is contingent on their gaining evidence of change in the learning outcomes of their students."[4] In other words, success breeds success. If we see evidence of incremental growth and perceive that this student is a capable learner, then our expectations and beliefs about his or her ability change. In the same way, the success that a student experiences begins to call in question any prior beliefs she may have had of herself as a learner. Each learning and assessment opportunity builds students' confidence and motivates them to achieve. So significant are a teacher's beliefs in a student's ability that Linda Darling-Hammond writes, "Students' willingness to commit to school and their own futures is interwoven with their perceptions about whether the society, their schools, and their teachers believe they are worthwhile investments—perceptions that enable them to invest in themselves."[5]

How to Solve the Grading Issues

While grading issues are complex and are not something that can be fixed overnight, classroom teachers can take several steps immediately to ensure that they are providing accurate and meaningful grades to all students, particularly ELLs.

One of the greatest disservices teachers can do to ELLs is not to grade them according to their language proficiency level. If a district has not tackled this subject, then it's up to ESL and content-area teachers to work together for a common solution. Here are some suggestions that may help (though, of course, be sure to discuss these ideas with your site administrator before you move forward with any of them):

- Work with your grade-level team to develop a supplemental grading report that can be included with the report card. See the sample in the Part Two Resources section.

- Decide how you will show student progress. Make sure you use the same language proficiency standards that you have been using to guide your instruction.

- Explain to parents that the report card reflects progress toward the ELA standards and the supplemental report reflects progress based on English language proficiency standards.

- Explain to students what these grades mean and how they can use the information to improve their performance.

- If your school or district is not ready to move forward with revising the existing grading policy for ELLs, convene a task force that can begin researching effective grading practices for ELLs. The following books are particularly valuable for members of a report card task force:

  Guskey, T., and Bailey, J. (2001) *Developing grading and reporting systems for student learning.* Thousand Oaks, CA: Corwin Press.

  O'Connor, K. (2010). *A repair kit for grading: Fifteen fixes for broken grades.* Needham Heights, MA: Allyn & Bacon.

  Reeves, D. (2011). *Elements of grading: A guide to effective practice.* Bloomington, IN: Solution Tree.

Chapter 9

Identifying Language Acquisition Levels

In This Chapter

- Accurately identifying and placing English learners
- Creating an ongoing language proficiency assessment
- Using the assessment results

Title III of the No Child Left Behind Act requires states to assess the language acquisition levels of ELLs annually. Certainly ESL teachers welcome the data from these assessments, but they are also frustrated by the fact that they do not receive the results in a timely manner. In fact, most teachers do not receive test reports until sometime between November and January. By then, a third of the school year has passed.

So how can students be placed in an appropriately leveled ESL class at the start of the year?

Creating Language Proficiency Assessments

In the elementary grades in schools with an ESL pull-out, in which students are pulled out of the regular classroom to receive daily ESL instruction, or push-in program, in which the ESL teacher comes into the regular classroom to provide ESL instruction within the context of the regular school day, typically the ESL teacher has previous experience with the students and can make an educated guess as to their appropriate placement. In some elementary schools, teachers teach ESL at the same time during the school day, which allows them to regroup their ELLs for leveled ESL instruction. In this case, teachers may turn to the previous grade level for information for grouping ELLs.

By middle and high school, ELLs usually have a class period devoted to ESL instruction. If the ESL department works collaboratively, they may be able to share some initial information pertaining to English language levels.

Many schools and districts have moved toward creating their own English language acquisition assessments in order to be able to monitor the progress that students are making in each of the four domains of speaking, writing, reading, and listening. Most of these assessments are observational protocols or performance-based assessments in which the teacher closely monitors the progress students are making. Due to the fact that most state English language proficiency standards are written in grade spans (K–2, 3–5, 6–8, and 9–12), these protocols include the language proficiency standards for each domain and follow students through that grade span (Figure 9.1). In the language proficiency

Grade 6

	First Trimester	Second Trimester	Third Trimester
Listening			
Speaking			
Reading			
Writing			
Signature			

Grade 7

	First Trimester	Second Trimester	Third Trimester
Listening			
Speaking			
Reading			
Writing			
Signature			

Grade 8

	First Trimester	Second Trimester	Third Trimester
Listening			
Speaking			
Reading			
Writing			
Signature			

Figure 9.1 Language Proficiency Assessment Example

How to Reach and Teach English Language Learners

assessment example in Figure 9.1, teachers use their professional judgment to determine a student's ongoing proficiency level in each of the domains. They then add the points to each domain and provide a signature confirming that the student has met the criteria for each level of proficiency and domain.

Using Assessment Results

Schools or districts that do not have a locally developed English language acquisition assessment should use the results from the state English language proficiency assessment.

Using the Part Two Resources section, particularly the English Learner Profile Sheet, the ESL teacher or English language coordinator can keep all mainstream teachers informed as to the levels of their English learners. Keep in mind that some teachers may not know which students in their classes are ELLs. This is particularly common in middle and high school, where content-area teachers may see more than ninety students a day.

ESL teachers should closely monitor their ELLs' progress and either modify their instruction accordingly or place them in a different level ESL class if they believe that the student has been misplaced. Although the master schedule typically drives instruction at the middle and high school levels, close consideration must be given to whether that schedule takes precedence over providing instruction to ELLs that helps propel them to the next levels of language acquisition and helps them avoid becoming long-term English learners.

Part Two Resources

Survey: Auditing Your English Language Learner Program

The purpose of an audit is to determine whether your school is providing the optimal program for its ELLs. Complete the audit as a staff or leadership team. Note that not all questions will apply to your particular situation. Discuss the implications of your findings and any possible modifications to your English language program.

Define your English learner population:

1. What is the demographic profile of your school or district?

2. What primary languages do the majority of your English learners speak?

3. How many English learners do you have in the school? How many at each grade level?

4. What is the average education level of the parents of English learners?

5. How many of your English learners were born in the United States?

6. What is the transiency rate of your English learner population?

   - High transiency

   - Low transiency

7. Do families of English learners participate in school functions?

   - Back-to-school night

   - Fall conferences

- Spring conferences
- Open house
- Parent–Teacher Association
- Field trips
- Classroom volunteer opportunities

Examine the effectiveness of your English learner program offerings:

8. What programs are currently offered to ELLs?

    - Bilingual
    - Bilingual, early exit
    - Bilingual, late exit
    - Dual immersion
    - English immersion
    - English mainstream

9. How many fully qualified and appropriately certified teachers to teach English learners do you have?

10. Do you have fully qualified bilingual or biliterate teachers to teach bilingual classes?

    - How many fully bilingual and biliterate teachers do you currently have?

11. Do you have any support staff available?

    - Bilingual or biliterate instructional assistants who can provide support for primary language instruction
    - An English language coordinator
    - Bilingual or biliterate parent volunteers
    - Parent volunteers who can assist in newcomer and bilingual classrooms to support primary language instruction

12. Examine at least three years of ELL data. What trends and patterns emerge?

13. Examine at least three years of annual measurable achievement objectives data. What trends and patterns emerge?

14. Examine local or benchmark assessment data. What trends and patterns emerge?

How to Reach and Teach English Language Learners

15. Examine the quality and effectiveness of your ESL programs:

Elementary Programs

- Push-in, taught by ESL teacher

- Pull-out, taught by ESL teacher

- Self-contained, with all levels taught simultaneously by a regular classroom teacher

- Leveled, with students receiving leveled ESL instruction taught by an appropriately certified teacher

Secondary Programs

- ESL class period driven by student needs

- ESL class period driven mostly by the master schedule

16. Assessment

- Teachers administer local English language acquisition assessment and regroup students accordingly.

- Students are placed in leveled ESL classes based on the results of the state English language proficiency assessment results.

Examine the knowledge level of your mainstream teaching staff:

17. Do teachers receive support in learning about and implementing high-impact strategies for ELLs?

18. Are mainstream teachers aware of the number of ELLs in their classrooms?

19. Are mainstream teachers aware of:

- Overall language acquisition levels?

- Language acquisition levels for each domain?

20. Mainstream teachers use information regarding ELL acquisition levels to plan differentiated lessons for their ELLs.

- Yes

- No

21. Mainstream teachers use information regarding ELL acquisition levels to plan differentiated assessment opportunities for their ELLs.

- Yes

- No

Sample Supplemental Grading Report

On the sample supplemental grading report in Figure 2R.1, each trimester parents and students receive information reflecting progress in each of the four domains: listening, speaking, reading, and writing. Teachers, therefore, assess language proficiency levels at least three times each year in addition to the state English language proficiency assessment.

Notice from Figure 2R.1 that teachers assign differentiated grades for reading and writing based on the student's level of language proficiency in each domain. In other words, the teacher bases the grades in these two domains on the standards for the language acquisition level of the student in reading and writing. In addition, the teacher can also report progress toward the ELA standards for that grade level, but the differentiated grade will help provide much more accurate feedback for the student.

Now consider the profile in Table 2R.1 for a typical ELL. Based on these levels, teachers find the corresponding English proficiency standards (or WIDA standards) in Table 2R.2 and use those to help determine a differentiated grade.

Using the results of our own language proficiency assessment, we can complete the sample supplemental grade report (see Figure 2R.2).

A parent, student, or teacher can tell from the scores in each of the language domains that the student has made progress in the areas of language proficiency writing and speaking. Although the student received differentiated grades, the areas of strength as well

Trimester			1st	2nd	3rd
English Mainstream ☐	Reading ELL Level				
	Reading Differentiated Grade				
English Immersion ☐	Writing ELL Level				
Bilingual English Development ☐	Writing Differentiated Grade				
	Listening Level				
	Speaking Level				

Figure 2R.1 Format for a Supplemental Grading Report

Table 2R.1 Sample Profile of an English Language Learner

	Trimester 1	Trimester 2	Trimester 3
Reading level	3	3	3
Writing level	2	2	3
Listening level	3	3	3
Speaking level	4	4	5

Table 2R.2 Sample English Language Proficiency Standards

Reading Level 3	Writing Level 2	Writing Level 3
• Use decoding skills and knowledge of both academic and social vocabulary to read independently. Recognize that some words have multiple meanings • Read text and use detailed sentences to explain orally the main ideas and details of informational text, literary text, and text in content areas.	• Write an increasing number of words and simple sentences appropriate for language arts and other content areas (math, science, history, and other social sciences). • Revise writing, with teacher assistance, to clarify meaning and improve the mechanics and organization. • Write expository compositions, such as descriptions, comparison and contrast, and problem and solution, that include a main idea and some details in simple sentences.	• Use more complex vocabulary and sentences appropriate for language arts and other content areas (math, science, history, and other social sciences). • Revise writing for appropriate word choice and organization with variation in grammatical forms and spelling. • Write brief expository compositions (description, comparison and contrast, cause and effect, and problem and solution) that include a thesis and some points of support.

as areas needing improvement are clear. Notice how the student's language proficiency level in writing changed from a 2 to a 3 in the third trimester, which caused a drop in the differentiated writing grade.

Academic Achievement Key

A = Exemplary   B = Proficient   C = Partially Proficient   N = Not Proficient

Trimester		1st	2nd	3rd
English Mainstream ☐	Reading ELL Level	3	3	3
	Reading Differentiated Grade	C	C	B
English Immersion ☐	Writing ELL Level	2	2	3
Bilingual English Development ☐	Writing Differentiated Grade	B	B	C
	Listening Level	3	3	3
	Speaking Level	4	4	5

Figure 2R.2 Completed Sample Grade Report

English Language Learner Profile Sheet

The English Language Learner Profile Sheet in Form 2R.1 can be filled-in by the ESL teacher and then shared with each of the content-area teachers. The information provided on the sheet helps teachers plan appropriate and culturally relevant lessons.

Form 2R.1 English Language Learner Profile Sheet

Student Name	Years in U.S. Schools	Overall English Learner Level	Listening	Speaking	Reading	Writing	Language	Literacy/ Proficiency Level in Native Language	Years in School Prior to Arrival in United States	Other Pertinent Information

Using the English Language Learner Profile Sheet

Who is responsible for completing the profile sheet, and who should receive it?

- Ideally the profile sheet should be completed by the ESL teacher or site English language coordinator as early in the year as possible. Schools can add this form to their student information system so that teachers could access this information electronically.

- The profile sheet should be distributed to all certificated staff who may encounter ELLs during the course of their day.

What purpose does the profile sheet serve?

- The profile sheet helps to ensure that all teachers know the students in their classrooms who have been designated ELL.

- Teachers can use the information to help develop differentiated instruction and assessments for ELLs.

What if the categories listed on the profile sheet do not meet our needs?

- This profile sheet is meant to get you started. Feel free to work with your staff to design a profile sheet that reflects the needs of your school or district. Here are some other characteristics that affect the rate of language acquisition that you might put on your profile sheet:[1]
  - Rural or urban background
  - Proficiency in conversational English
  - Proficiency in academic and written English
  - Age
  - Age of enrollment in U.S. schools
  - Family circumstances and responsibilities
  - Living situation
  - History of mobility (Olsen, 2010)
  - Parents' employment and work schedule
  - Immigration or refugee status (Olsen, 2010)
  - History of trauma
  - Family legal status

How to Reach and Teach English Language Learners

- Family educational history
- Student's birth order in the family
- Religious beliefs and practices
- Continued contact with country of origin and language (Tabors, 1997)
- Gender roles and assumptions
- Aspirations and expectations
- Interests, talents, and skills
- Funds of knowledge and community support

Discussion Questions

1. What instructional programs do we offer?
2. Are these the best possible programs given our resources?
3. Are these the best possible programs for our population of English learners?
4. How do we assess English learners?
5. Do our English learners stay in the same-level ESL class all year, or do we use our own assessments to place them?
6. Do teachers know how to differentiate assessments in the content areas so that English learners of all levels can show mastery of content?
7. How do we grade English learners? Is the grading policy fair?
8. If our district won't change the policy, can we provide more meaningful information for parents and students?

Part Three

Reaching English Language Learners

The chapters in Part Three clearly define how to create a school environment that fosters high levels of achievement of all students, including English language learners.

Chapter 10

Lowering the Affective Filter

In This Chapter

- Establishing a low affective filter environment in your classroom

- Strategies for creating an environment in which English learners can excel

- A peek into two classrooms

The natural approach theory to language acquisition proposes that we learn best when we acquire a new language in a manner similar to the way we learned our native language: naturally and through regular interaction with others proficient in the language.[1] The theory postulates that in the natural process of language acquisition, students acquire language best when they are provided with comprehensible input in an environment with a low affective filter. The *affective filter* is defined as a screen of emotion that can block language acquisition or learning if it keeps the users from being too self-conscious or too embarrassed to take risks when they speak. In fact,

Krashen writes, "The best methods are . . . those that supply 'comprehensible input' in low anxiety situations, containing messages that students really want to hear. These methods do not force early production in the second language, but allow students to produce when they are 'ready', recognizing that improvement comes from supplying communicative and comprehensible input, and not from forcing and correcting production."[2] *Comprehensible input* refers to input that is at the right level for an ELL to remain engaged in the learning. In other words, it is neither too challenging nor too easy.

Establishing a Low Affective Filter

If, as Krashen theorizes, the learner's emotional state or attitudes are part of an adjustable screen that allows or impedes input necessary to acquire language, then it follows that a low affective filter is imperative to learning since it blocks less of the input.

Krashen and Terrell identify three types of affective variables related to second language acquisition: self-confidence, motivation, and low anxiety. They conclude that learners who have self-confidence and a positive self-image tend to be more successful, highly motivated learners who outperform those with low motivation, and a low-anxiety environment is more conducive to second language acquisition.[3]

While Krashen's theories are still among the most respected in the field of second language acquisition, there has been much need for concrete strategies that lower the affective filter—strategies that help create a stress-free environment where mistakes are accepted as part of the learning process and where students can engage in communication. Here are some ways to create a classroom environment that supports natural acquisition in a low affective filter environment:

- Use objects, photographs, or illustrations that reinforce spoken or written words and make the content you are presenting comprehensible.

- Employ gestures for added emphasis and to provide clues to meaning.

- Adjust and simplify your speech: speak slowly and enunciate; use longer natural pauses, shorter sentences, fewer pronouns, and simpler syntax; and repeat words or phrases. Remember that the key is to simplify, not water down, the content.

- Stress high-frequency vocabulary words.

- Clarify the meaning of words or phrases in context.

- Use fewer idioms.

- Use cooperative learning.

- Be enthusiastic and maintain a low anxiety level.

Lowering the Affective Filter

Although establishing a low affective filter classroom environment is important for all English learners, this section focuses on ELLs at the beginning levels of language acquisition since a low affective filter is particularly important to the development of basic English skills. We begin with a section on helping you assess whether you have all the pieces in place to implement this strategy.

Ensuring the Environment Is Conducive to Learning

Take a moment to answer the following questions about your own classroom environment and then work with your colleagues to reflect on your practice as a team:

- *Are all of the students in my ESL class placed appropriately?* If they were placed based on the state's ELL assessment, consider how recently that assessment was administered. Remember that students are in level 1 for a relatively short period of time (up to six months), and having students misplaced raises the anxiety level of those students who are truly level 1, especially if they feel that other students may be more proficient in English than they are. Use the English Language Learner Profile worksheet in the Part Two Resources section to help you ensure appropriate placement of English learners.
- *Are all teachers aware of the levels of each ELL in their classroom?* Is a process in place to disseminate the most current ELL level information to all content-area teachers? ELLs most likely spend the majority of their day with mainstream content teachers learning math, science, social studies, and reading/language arts. Teachers need to know which students in their classes, if any, are ELLs so that they can work to establish a low affective filter for them. Use the information in the Part Two Resources section, particularly the English Language Learner Profile Sheet, to organize your students by level and help you disseminate this information to all teachers on your team who have beginning-level ELLs.
- *Am I differentiating my content especially for beginning-level ELLs?* Once you have identified your beginning-level ELLs and disseminated that information to all teachers who work with those students, ensure that you are appropriately differentiating tasks, assignments, and questions for any beginning-level students. Remember that asking students to produce language before they are ready to do so raises their anxiety. Beginning-level students should be labeling, drawing pictures and diagrams, and writing one-word or short-phrase responses. When questioning them, you should be asking them to point or indicate with gestures their responses or preferences. (The chapters in Part Five offer more strategies appropriate to beginning-level ELLs in your grade span and content area.)

Strategies for Lowering the Affective Filter

Use this list of strategies as a starting point, and brainstorm other strategies that can help you lower the affective filter for your English learners:

- Take the time to get to know your students. Learn about their countries of origin and cultural traditions.

- Find ways to include information about your students' countries of origin and culture in your lessons.

- Pronounce your students' names correctly. This is part of their cultural identity, so honor them by asking them to teach you how to pronounce their names.

- Use total physical response (TPR) as much as possible to help ELLs access the content you are teaching, whether that content is ESL or math. A key component of the affective filter theory states that we should be making content comprehensible for students so that they can better access the information we are trying to teach them. (Chapter Sixteen provides more detailed information on using TPR effectively in your classroom.)

- Give students the opportunity to share something about themselves or their culture with the entire class. This doesn't need to involve speaking if they are not comfortable enough yet to speak to an audience. Instead, they can create collages with pictures and information about their native countries that they post and share with the class. Opportunities for students to share their culture can be ongoing.

- Establish an environment of respect within the classroom. This involves more than saying, "We value diversity," or "We respect everyone." It means deliberately working to create an environment in which each student feels validated, respected, and valued, regardless of language acquisition level or country of origin. As the teacher, we need to model respect on a daily basis and always remember that students are watching our cues.

Creating a low affective filter is a process. Your ELLs will be more likely to take risks with English when you have worked to develop an environment where they feel safe.

A Peek into Two Classrooms

The two scenarios that follow allow us to take a closer look at instruction for English learners. Note not only the implementation of strategies but also the affective filter in each of these classrooms and the strategies each teacher uses to maintain a low affective filter.

Scenario 1

Mrs. Lee has taught at least one section of ELL math for the past ten years and especially enjoys working with beginning-level students because it's so gratifying to see their progress. She has recently received professional development on research-based strategies for math instruction. She heard the message loud and clear: students need vocabulary instruction, and she knows that this is especially true of ELLs. She decides to add a math vocabulary notebook to all of her math classes.

She also decides that she will teach her students a structured method for note taking, since she learned at another professional development institute that this is a high-impact strategy. That's enough to sell her on it.

On the first day of the next unit of instruction for eighth graders, she writes the vocabulary words on the board and asks students to look up the words in the glossary and write a definition in their vocabulary notebooks. She also asks them to apply the new vocabulary by writing a sentence using each word. The teacher uses Popsicle sticks with students' names on them to call on students to read their definitions and sentences out loud to the class.

She then explains note taking to her students and walks them through the process of setting up their paper. She asks students to help each other and work together. Using an overhead projector, Mrs. Lee walks through three examples and has students record the notes she's writing on the overhead in appropriate format. She closes the lesson by asking students if they have any questions before they start their independent practice.

Students then get to work on their problem set. She encourages them to use their vocabulary notebooks and notes to help them complete the assignment successfully. Students work independently. When they ask each other questions, Mrs. Lee reminds them that they are supposed to be working independently.

Scenario 2

Mr. De Rosa also teaches ELL math. He attended the same workshop on vocabulary and note taking that Mrs. Lee did. Like Mrs. Lee, he is always looking for new ways to ensure academic success for his English learners. He loves learning about new strategies, then implementing those strategies in a way that makes sense for his student population.

He introduces vocabulary notebooks to his eighth graders by showing the students an example that illustrates what he expects their work to look like. He opens math class by listing the vocabulary for the lesson. Students copy the words and complete a graphic organizer that includes many strategies, including drawing pictures, diagrams, or writing single words or phrases that help them define the word and remember it. He encourages students to help each other by explaining new concepts or vocabulary to each other in their native language. Mr. De Rosa has some old math textbooks and workbooks in class that have been in his cupboards for many years collecting dust. He allows students who'd rather not draw to cut pictures out of these books and glue those images next to their vocabulary words.

Next, he continues with today's concept by putting a problem on the board that is just above the students' current level of understanding. He has the students open up their notebooks and copy the problem. In groups, they work to come to a solution, using their native language support with textbooks and primary language explanations by their classmates. He encourages them to use their vocabulary notebooks to label the steps of their solution. He tells them it is acceptable for the labels to be one- or two-word phrases, and spelling or grammar does not count. Students can come up as a group and, using the document camera, show the steps they followed. Groups are given a few minutes to practice their presentations. Mr. De Rosa has reinforced that mistakes are part of the learning process and regularly reminds them of this. It is amazing to see all of the different ways that students have arrived at a solution and the way that they are able to demonstrate their math knowledge given the fact that they have limited English skills.

Finally, Mr. De Rosa provides a word bank and asks students to use it and sentence frames that he supplies to write complete sentences reflecting the process they followed to solve the problem. This new note-taking strategy also allows students to use words or images to represent their new learning graphically. They are then given the opportunity to read their sentences and share their graphic representations with a partner. Any student who would like to share his or her work aloud to the entire class is encouraged to do so.

This allows students to hear and process several different representations of the new learning.

Mr. De Rosa shows them a few additional examples that they will encounter in the homework and has students copy those examples into their notes. Students then open the textbook and begin working on independent practice. They are encouraged to work with a partner, use their vocabulary notebooks, and use their notes.

 Questions to Consider

1. Both teachers used strategies that they thought would lower the affective filter. Was one teacher more successful at accomplishing it than the other? If so, which one, and why was this so?

2. How did knowledge of second language acquisition learning theories help one teacher modify those strategies in a way that ensured the success of beginning-level ELLs?

3. How important is it for all teachers who work with ELLs, not just ESL teachers, to have an understanding of second language acquisition theories and strategies? What implications does this understanding have for the quality of instruction that ELLs are receiving in your district, school, or classroom?

Chapter 11

Connecting with Families of English Language Learners

In This Chapter

- The importance of connecting with families

- Making families feel welcome on campus

- Strategies for getting parents involved in their children's education

Connecting with families of ELLs is every bit as important as connecting with the learners themselves in the classroom. The Southwest Educational Development Laboratory found "compelling, research-based evidence that when schools and families work together, student achievement spikes, particularly in low-performing schools."[1] Involving parents who speak limited English, are intimidated by their child's school, or work multiple jobs is a significant challenge. Some schools have found a way of connecting with families by offering social services, including counseling and health care.[2]

Many families of English learners have come to view the school as a resource for helping them navigate their way through our systems and social services.

Epstein and colleagues identified six practices that further foster parent and community partnerships:

1. Assist families with parenting skills.

2. Improve communication with families.

3. Increase opportunities for families to volunteer at school.

4. Help increase family involvement in student learning at home.

5. Ensure that families play a role in school decision making.

6. Increase collaboration with the community.[3]

Where to Begin

If you are not sure where to begin, it may be worth the effort to survey your community. The information you gather can help identify areas that parents need help with, topics that they may be interested in learning about, and volunteer work that they may be interested in doing. You can also find out how welcome and safe parents feel on your campus. This information can help you structure an effective school and community partnership. Work with your Parent–Teacher Association and leadership team for ideas on communicating with families and involving them in the decision-making process. (For other ideas, see the Part Three Resources section.)

Making Parents and Families Feel Welcome

Before moving forward with implementing programs that increase parental involvement, ensure that parents feel welcome on campus. Parental attendance at school events will not be significant until they do. For the most part, we all like to think that our campuses are welcoming for all parents. However, a deeper look may reveal that parents from all cultural backgrounds may not feel welcome.

Begin by making an honest assessment of family outreach at your school. Keep in mind that parents who may be in the country illegally may have a sincere fear of school officials. Although this is a touchy subject, ensure that parents and families know that the role of the school is to educate their children, not to play a role in law or immigration enforcement.

Ideas

- Understand the population and the dynamics of the immigrant families you serve. Keep in mind the changing demographics of the community, and make sure that your campus is being responsive to those changes.

- Understand that culture, language, and identity are deeply connected to and play a large part in the academic development of ELLs and other minority students. Make sure that images on posters and bulletin boards reflect the demographics of the community.

- If recent changes in demographics have caught your school and community by surprise, search for ways to become a culturally inclusive school. If your school lacks resources and your staff needs professional development, make that a top priority.

- Appoint a family liaison or other community representative to work with families. The best way to connect with your community is to appoint someone to serve as an intermediary between the school and the community. This person can play an integral role in establishing communication with the community by planning and organizing educational events and leading research into the ethnography of the community to help teaching staff learn about the cultural backgrounds of their students. This person can also reach out to parents of different cultural backgrounds and encourage them to play an active role in their child's education.

- Keep in mind that parents are busy people and may hold multiple jobs. When planning school events, ensure that you are scheduling them at different hours of the day in an effort to reach everyone. Parents will appreciate your consideration.

- Make your campus a hub of activity so that parents and families feel compelled to be a part of the school community.

- Make use of community resources for translation and communication services. A proportion of your parent population may be illiterate or have minimal literacy skills. Keep school communications brief and to the point so that all parents can understand the information. Use vehicles other than Web sites or newsletters to keep parents informed; for example, use phone systems to send voice messages to families informing them of upcoming events. If possible, record these messages in multiple languages so that all parents will understand the information.

- Teach parents how to partner with teachers and be involved in their child's education. For many cultures, the teacher represents the pinnacle of society. To imply that parents can be partners with teachers in educating their child may be a completely foreign idea to them. Many of them do not believe that they have the skills to play a contributing role in the education of their children. It is up to us to validate the skills they do have and to show them how they can use those skills to help their children succeed. My mother, who had very limited literacy skills, attended every conference and school function and made sure that my brothers and I had a quiet place to do our homework. We need to encourage parents to play a role in helping to educate their children, however limited they may believe their contribution may be.

- Provide translation services when planning important school events such as back-to-school night, open house, or parent conferences. Also provide child-care services.

- Be an advocate for underserved families. For many families, particularly those in high-poverty areas, the neighborhood school is the only public institution they have regular contact with. Be sure to have information on hand in multiple languages for public services in the community.

- Host a "school field trip" where families of newcomers can come to the school and receive orientation information. Have bilingual students serve as student ambassadors who lead the orientation for families who speak the same primary language that they do. Students as young as second graders can play the role of student ambassador with proper training.

Educational Opportunities for Parents

Using information gathered from the parent survey, begin planning educational opportunities for parents based on their needs and interests. Look to state departments of education, the U.S. Department of Education, and the National Parent Teacher Association for curriculum and materials.[4] For any of these educational opportunities for parents, consider offering child-care services:

- Offer classes in English, technology training, health and nutrition, and parenting, which includes getting children ready for school.

- Particularly for parents at the secondary level, offer parenting skills for the teenage years, a series of family nights featuring such topics as gangs, drugs, alcohol, safe sex, bullying, and violence.[5] Keep in mind that some of these topics are very uncomfortable for many cultures to confront. While many parents struggle with such topics, some immigrant parents may have been raised in rural areas and may have limited understanding themselves in addition to not being comfortable with speaking openly about such topics. Be mindful of these considerations as you plan events.

- Consider hosting some of these events within the community, at local church auditoriums, Masonic Temples, or other local community gathering places. By leaving the school campus and taking our show on the road, we promote the idea that we are part of the community as well.

  - Invite parents to participate in family nights such as these:

  Family Culture Night. Establish a date when you will come together at a school site to recognize the cultures represented by the families in your school. Resist the temptation to have a "multicultural" event where each classroom chooses a different country to represent. The point here is to publicly recognize and celebrate the cultures of the students in your classrooms.

  Family Reading Night. Many parents are not literate. Take the time to establish a relationship with your parent community so that they feel comfortable sharing this type of very personal information with you. Share with these families the strategies they can use to help their children develop strong reading and comprehension skills. A common way to organize the evening could include a time where parents and students are in separate rooms learning different strategies and then a time when parents and children come together to practice the strategies they learned under the guidance of a teacher. A great way to create excitement is to give a book to each family that attends.

  Family Math Night. Family Math Night should be about finding ways to do math in fun ways at home with children. It should also focus on introducing parents who were educated in another country the steps typically followed in the United States to solve problems such as multidigit multiplication and long division. I often had parents ask me to teach them how to solve problems the way they had learned so that they could help their students at home. Take advantage of these opportunities and ask parents to come to class one day to teach everyone the strategy. By doing this, you not only connect with parents on a different level but also instill a sense of pride in parents and students alike. Like other family nights, make sure you schedule both a daytime and an evening session. Take the time to create and share strategies for reproducible manipulatives such as pattern blocks and algebra tiles. This will ensure that students are practicing concepts at home that will help them in school.

Family Science Night. Of all the family nights, I believe that Family Science Night may be one of the most exciting for everyone, parents and students alike. Use Web sites such as www.stevespangler.com to help bring science alive for your families and students. You can also find excellent Web sites offering resources for hosting your own Family Science Night. Have something that families get to take home with them to practice the science concepts they learned. Leaving with a "science experiment in a bag" is exciting and motivating to parents and students alike.

Not only are these events fun for the whole family, they are also a fun and engaging way to teach parents how to help support their children's learning at home. Offer translation services, or, if possible, host the nights in multiple languages. (See the Part Three Resources section for family night planning resources.) Also, make sure that you provide child-care services. It may be necessary to offer morning and evening sessions for parents who do not work at traditional nine-to-five jobs.

The Importance of Cultural Connections

There is no doubt that growing up in a bilingual, bicultural home helped shape my attitudes and beliefs about the world around me. As an adult woman, I can say that I feel that I am a perfect combination of these two worlds, able to seamlessly switch back and forth between both languages and cultures; however, it was not always easy. Living immersed in one culture at home meant that I needed to learn how to function within the rules of a different culture at school and that I would also need to learn to navigate my way through a world that was initially as foreign to me as it was to my parents. I often found myself feeling torn between two worlds, not knowing quite where I fit in. For example, my Mexican culture dictated traditional values and roles when it came to girls and boys, but

American culture seemed to contradict many of these values. I can remember my family sitting at the dinner table and my father explaining to my two brothers and me that the most important thing we could do is get a good education. Armed with that education, we could accomplish anything we set our minds to. This seemed to be in direct contradiction to the more traditional role, which dictated that a woman's place was in the home. Mixed cultural messages such as these, particularly those regarding the roles of girls and boys, are only a small part of the challenges we need to address when working with students from diverse cultural backgrounds.

Ladson-Billings writes that culturally relevant teachers use their own students' cultures as a vehicle for learning.[1] In doing so, we validate the cultures and cultural practices of our students. We also reinforce for students the importance of maintaining their culture as part of who they are. Trueba echoes this sentiment: "If children manage to retain a strong cultural self-identity and maintain a sense of belonging to their socio-cultural community, they seem to achieve well in school."[2]

Teachers should also share their own cultural heritage and how that culture is part of their daily lives. Every one of us has a cultural background, and sharing that background helps students connect with us and helps to set a tone of acceptance in the classroom.

Funds of Knowledge

Funds of knowledge are defined by researchers Luis Moll, Cathy Amanti, Deborah Neff, and Norma González as "the historically accumulated and culturally developed bodies of knowledge and skills essential for household or individual functioning and well-being."[3] In other words, every family has a fund of knowledge that encompasses its history and culture, and the family members pull from this fund in order to function and thrive. González, Moll, and Amanti encourage teachers to shed the role of expert and become learners about the students and cultures represented in their classrooms.[4] This process allows teachers to view their students and families in a new light. They come to understand that their students have rich cultural and cognitive resources, and they begin to use that information to design culturally responsive lessons that are meaningful to them and tap their prior knowledge. Any information that a teacher collects is considered the student's fund of knowledge.[5]

Learning about students at this depth requires us to leave the school campus, venture out into the community, and visit our students at home. We must be open and willing to not just learn *about* but also to learn *from* and *with* their families. This strategy may be of particular importance for schools experiencing a surge in immigrant students or changing demographics. Because most of us were not raised in the same cultures as these new students, our responsibility is to take on the role of researcher and learn all we can about our students. Taking the time to learn about, know, and understand their historical, cultural, and personal situations helps us build bridges between home and the classroom and allows us to incorporate out students' funds of knowledge into our instruction.[6]

Connecting with Families

Connecting with the families of students on this level has many positive outcomes, one being the negation of such things as the cultural deficit theory, which is pervasive in so many schools and classrooms across the country. The cultural deficit model contends that immigrant and minority cultural values are dysfunctional, and thus the cause of low achievement among these groups of students. Although great efforts have been made to combat such inaccurate and misleading ideas about English learners, many misconceptions that keep the cultural deficit model going persist in schools across the country.

Recent research has also shown that some secondary teachers have developed other inaccurate perceptions regarding ELLs. J.R. Reeves, for example, discovered the following misconceptions about ELLs that secondary teachers in her study held: that ELLs should be able to acquire English within two years and that they should avoid using their native language as they acquire English.[7]

It has become exceedingly clear from the research that the rate of second language acquisition is dependent on a number of factors, including age, years of schooling in the child's native country, environment, and first-language proficiency.[8] Although research has been unable to determine the exact number of years that it should take a student to acquire language, most research confirms that in most cases it could take more than seven years.[9]

Although the secondary teacher's perception that two years is a sufficient amount of time for full-language proficiency is not supported by research, Reeves found that a disturbingly high number of secondary teachers in her study held that belief. A major concern is that a misconception such as this one may lead teachers to make inaccurate conclusions concerning the English learners' language ability, intelligence, or motivation, which in turn feeds the cultural deficit model.

Intimate understanding of our students' funds of knowledge prevents us from accepting or believing that they are not acquiring English at a fast enough rate because they are lazy or unmotivated. Spending time in their homes and learning from their families and them confirms that though our ELLs may be different culturally, their hopes and desires are no different from our own.

 Questions to Consider

1. Do I validate my students by using their cultures as a vehicle for instruction?

2. Do students feel a sense of pride in their cultural identity? If not, what can I do to change that?

3. Do I share my own cultural heritage and practices with my students?

4. Does my instruction emphasize respect for and acceptance of students of diverse cultural backgrounds?

Ideas

- Request professional development opportunities to build your own confidence in being culturally responsive.

- Work as a school or district to ensure that students feel welcomed and accepted on your campus.

- Invite members of the community to your campus who can provide positive cultural role models for your students.

How to Reach and Teach English Language Learners

Part Three Resources

Planning Resources for Family Nights

Sample Parent Letter

FAMILY CULTURE NIGHT

Date:

Time:

Location:

Over the past few weeks, students have been working very hard to learn about their culture and decide how to introduce the rest of the community to that culture.

Come join us as we celebrate the many cultures represented in our school.

Child-care services will be provided.

Parent Education Planning Checklist

Based on the results of the parent survey, choose a topic:

- ☐ Health and nutrition
- ☐ Preparing your child for school
- ☐ Basic computer class
- ☐ Intermediate computer class
- ☐ E-mail training
- ☐ Basic English
- ☐ Preparing to help your child apply to college

Based on the results of the parent survey, choose a topic that involves parents meeting over several weeks:

- ☐ Basic English skills
- ☐ Parenting classes

Identify the topics you'd like to cover as a series over several weeks:

- ☐ Gangs
- ☐ Bullying
- ☐ Alcohol
- ☐ Drugs
- ☐ Violence
- ☐ Sex

Other considerations are funding, staff, materials, location, child care, translation, and flyers (students can help design flyers and translate them).

Family Night Planning Checklist

- ☐ Secure funding for events such as family nights by including them in your school plan.
- ☐ Assign a family night representative to the Parent–Teacher Association or site council. This person will head the committee that organizes these events.
- ☐ Decide on the dates.
- ☐ Work with teaching staff to organize and promote the event.
- ☐ Invite students and their families to participate.
- ☐ Secure child-care services for the event.
- ☐ Contact local businesses to donate supplies.
- ☐ Contact community members to provide translation services.
- ☐ Train students, particularly those who are bilingual, to help provide translation services.

Family Reading Night Parent Resources for Elementary Schools

These reading strategies make a good handout for parents.

Before-Reading Strategies

- Good readers make predictions about what will happen in a book. Take your child on a "walk" through the book and look at pictures, headings, and any other clues.

- Make a prediction. Have your child tell you what he or she thinks will happen. Add a prediction of your own.

- Good readers ask questions about the story before they read it. Ask your child what questions he or she might have about the story before reading it.

During-Reading Strategies

- Good readers monitor their comprehension. Make sure you remind your child to stop and reread if needed. Model this strategy yourself.

- Good readers stop and ask clarifying questions if there is a word or idea they don't understand. Modeling this strategy for your child is the best way to teach him or her how to do it. Think out loud as you ask your question—for example, "I don't know what the word *furious* means. Let's keep reading and see if we can discover what it means." Another strategy is to teach your child how to use a dictionary.

After-Reading Strategies

- Good readers summarize what they've read. Have your child tell you what he or she just read about.

Encourage parents with limited literacy skills or those who don't speak or read in English to read books in their primary language or have their children read to them. Train parents during Family Reading Night how to use these strategies regardless of their literacy levels.

Family Night Parent Resources for Secondary School

These reading strategies make a good handout for parents.

- Make sure that your child reads every night.

- Provide a quiet place for reading.

- Visit the local library and help your child select books.
- Remind your child about what good readers do:
  - *Predict.* Based on the illustrations, titles, and subheads, what do I think this story will be about?
  - *Question.* What questions do I think will be answered in this chapter?
  - *Clarify.* Are there any ideas or words that I don't understand?
  - *Summarize.* How can I summarize in my own words what I just read?
- Make it a nightly routine to ask your child to share a summary of what he or she has read.

Discussion Questions

1. Do all classrooms have a low affective filter in which English learners feel safe and encouraged to take risks?

2. What strategies can we use that will help students feel safe, with low levels of anxiety within the classroom?

3. In what ways are we connecting with families?

4. Do we have a high rate of parent involvement? If not, what could we do as a school to encourage parents to participate more?

5. Do teachers know their population of English learners? Could we benefit from getting out into the community to develop funds of knowledge?

6. Do any of our teachers subscribe to the cultural deficit model? If so, how can developing funds of knowledge help us combat this mistaken notion?

7. Can we host a Family Culture Night to help parents and students feel they are part of the school community?

8. Would we be open to hosting Family Reading, Math, or Science Nights to teach parents how to help their child at home?

9. Are we able to provide any other parent education opportunities that will bring parents to our campus?

Part Four

Teaching English Language Learners

The chapters in Part Four focus on helping teachers identify best practices for English language learners. They explore strategies for engaging students in the use of the four domains of language—listening, speaking, reading, and writing—every day and in every content area, sheltered instruction, and English as a Second Language.

Chapter 13

What We Do Matters

The Importance of High-Quality Instruction

In This Chapter

- Research on the impact of high-quality teaching
- Action research and how it can help us identify the strategies that work best with our students
- Conducting action research

After identifying English language learners and taking some time to identify their current levels of English language proficiency, it is important to give special consideration to the best ways to teach and help them achieve at each of those levels. Although there is no question that teacher instincts and judgment play a significant role in instructional decisions, research has shown that they're not enough. With the advent of standards and accountability has come a shift toward using data as a basis for instructional decisions versus relying solely on instincts and professional judgment.

There is no doubt that the number of challenges teachers face can leave them believing that there is little they can do to change the trajectory of the lives of their students. Recent bodies of evidence illustrate that this is far from true, however. In his recent book, *Visible Learning*, John Hattie writes, "Take two students of the same ability and it matters less to which school they go than the influences of the teacher, curricular program, or teaching they experience."[1] More than ever before, we know and can quantify the fact that what teachers do matters. Hattie shows empirically that everything teachers do has an impact on student achievement, but some practices work better than others. He challenges us to change our question from "What works?" to "What works best?" in an effort to sort out those strategies that have an effect that can be measured.

Asking what works best is especially critical to closing the achievement gap that exists for so many ELLs. In fact, the most recent information on on-time graduation rates for students of color is dismal. According to *Education Week*, only 55 percent of Hispanic students graduate on time from high school, and students from low-income families drop out of high school at six times the rate of their high-income peers.[2] As we saw in Part One, many ELLs fall into these two categories and are counting on us to prevent them from becoming a statistic.

Action Research to Identify High-Impact Strategies

Although there is currently not a large body of research on best practices specific to what works with ELLs, we can apply what we know about second language acquisition, take those best practices, and discuss implementing those strategies within the context of second language acquisition. For example, if we are implementing the use of Cornell Notes based on the research that this is a high-impact strategy, as Mrs. Lee and Mr. De Rosa did in Chapter Ten, we must go one step further and decide the best way to implement this strategy for ELLs and, more specifically, how that strategy may look different depending on the level of ELL we are working with. Think back to those scenarios in Chapter Ten: Do you think it was the high-yield strategy or the differentiation of that strategy that had a positive impact on student achievement? It is also important to consider how differentiating the strategies contributed to a lower affective filter for students. It has already been established how important both of these elements are to the success of English learners.

If, as John Hattie and so many other researchers say, what teachers do matters, then research specific to ELLs must be conducted to help us identify those high-yield strategies. Until such a body of evidence exists, we can engage in the next best thing: conducting action research within our own schools and classrooms.

In our constant effort to cover as much content as possible, we seldom take a moment to stop and ask if what we are doing is working. In a landmark study, Douglas Reeves has helped to establish that race, ethnicity, and socioeconomic status need no longer be predictors of academic success. One of the best practices that the schools in this study engage in is the constructive use of data. Teachers rely on a cyclical process of collecting and analyzing data to determine the effectiveness of the strategies they use to teach. This reflective process allows them identify the cause data, or adult actions, that yielded the results.[3]

When teachers of ELLs use this process, they not only identify the practices that bring about the best results but, more important, can help others replicate those results. Imagine how powerful this practice would be for Mrs. Lee and Mr. De Rosa. Rather than focus on the teacher, we look at the results of their instruction and then identify the causes for success. Those are the practices to replicate.

Conducting Action Research

The best way to conduct action research is with a willing team of colleagues who are committed to the process of uncovering the best practices to replicate. Action research is not an end in itself but rather a process of inquiry in which teachers analyze the results of their teaching and in so doing identify the causes of those results. It is a process that changes the nature of teachers' questions from focusing on what was taught to whether students learned.

The process that follows is based on the work of Larry Ainsworth, a senior professional development associate for the Leadership and Learning Center and author of *Power Standards* and *"Unwrapping" the Standard,* and has been modified with the needs of English learners in mind:[4]

1. Identify a power (that is, a priority) standard that English learners need to master.[5]

2. Cross-reference the English language proficiency standard with a priority standard from the content area you are teaching. (ESL teachers focus on the language proficiency standards, which are their content standards.)

3. "Unwrap" both standards by identifying the concepts and skills within each prioritized standard and determining the Bloom's level of each skill. This process not only helps clarify the standard but also helps to ensure that all teachers have a common definition of proficiency for the prioritized standard.

4. Create a common formative pre- and postassessment to clarify proficiency further.

5. Plan appropriate instruction that will lead to proficiency on the standards. This model of backward mapping helps to align instruction and ensure that every teacher at each grade level or content area is teaching the standard to the same level.

6. Administer the common formative preassessment.

7. Refine the instruction and differentiate according to the results of the common formative preassessment.

8. Engage in a cycle of teaching informed by the results of formative assessments along the way to ensure high levels of learning for all students.

9. Administer the common formative postassessment. Analyze the results, while staying focused on the impact of instructional strategies.

10. Repeat the process with each subsequent prioritized standard.

This cyclical process yields a body of evidence that informs instruction for teachers about the strategies that work best with a specific population of students. Although the process is driven by research-based practices, a team of teachers can identify the specific practices as well as differentiation that work best for their students. In the end, this type of action research has a positive impact on both teaching and learning for English learners as teachers build a body of evidence that can be used and refined as the population evolves. Students benefit from the results of targeted and informed instructional practice.

Chapter 14

Using the Four Domains of Language in Teaching

In This Chapter

- A review of the four language domains
- The four language domains in action
- An introduction to the fifth domain: thinking

We have seen that language acquisition progresses through five predictable levels and how teachers can use knowledge of those levels to plan highly engaging differentiated lessons by appropriately implementing the strategies to fit the needs of the students. The four language domains—listening, speaking, reading, and writing—are not to be confused with language acquisition levels. When we look at these domains, we realize that they permeate our lives and almost everything that we do. Undoubtedly listening and speaking may be the two more dominant language domains, but there is no denying that reading and writing contribute to and enrich our lives in terms of learning.

The Domains in Detail

Each of the four domains is typically defined in terms of being a productive or receptive skill, although this may often depend on whether the language is being used in a social or academic context.

Listening

Listening is considered a receptive skill, but in school settings, when learners need to listen for a purpose, it becomes an active skill. Although listening may seem like second nature, students must be guided in how to listen actively. The best way to do that is to involve ELLs in purposeful listening skills development. Teachers can help students develop these skills by providing questions and prompts prior to a listening task that help focus the student. Initially, teachers can develop these questions and prompts. Then as the students become more adept, they can begin developing their own. By doing so, we teach them that listening is a skill and that the best way to improve that skill is to practice it as much as possible. Socially (and at home, as some of us can attest to), students may choose to practice selective listening, where they do not lend the same level of attention and focus over a period of time. Students need to learn that when it comes to academic language (more formally, cognitive academic language proficiency), the listening skills they need to call on are much different from those they use when engaged in social language (the basic interpersonal communication skills) listening skills.

Speaking

Speaking is a productive skill. Although it is the domain that comes most naturally in the form of oral language, ELLs, and particularly newcomers, may hesitate to engage in oral language at the earliest stages of language acquisition. Creating an accepting and nonthreatening environment with a low affective filter is an important step in setting the stage for newcomers to begin to attempt to speak the language. Production of oral language should never be forced and rushed. For ELLs at least at level 3 (speech emergence), speaking will be much more natural than it is for those at levels 1 or 2; in fact, many of them may have developed high levels of social language and may thus sound much like native speakers, especially out on the playground or in other social settings. Students at this level and above need to engage in oral communication in a variety of situations, for a variety of purposes, and in a broad array of settings to build their oral language proficiency. Encouraging them to speak and interact during academic content instruction in order to build their academic vocabulary ensures that we build both strong academic oral language as well as social language.

Reading

Reading, like listening, is also considered a receptive language domain; however, it requires active processing skills in order for comprehension to take place. Reading, like the other

How to Reach and Teach English Language Learners

domains, also develops at different rates depending on whether it is social or academic reading. Reading skills involved in reading an invitation, menu, or cable guide involve minimal processing, whereas the reading skills called on in reading a historical novel or a math textbook demand high levels of comprehension. At its highest levels, reading encompasses processing, interpreting, and evaluating written language, symbols, and text with understanding and fluency.

Writing

Writing is a productive skill that has been shown by research study after research study to improve academic achievement dramatically. To write about something is to comprehend it, and so writing is a cognitively demanding skill that requires high levels of understanding and knowledge. We can encourage beginning-level ELLs to express meaning through drawings, symbols, or simple text consisting of short phrases or simple words. Keep in mind that if they attended school in their native country prior to attending U.S. schools, they may come with writing styles influenced by their home cultures. As ELLs enter level 3 and higher, they can begin to improve their facility of using written communication for a variety of purposes and audiences. Again, writing research reports and other content-heavy assignments requires high levels of academic and content vocabulary.

Engaging Students Using the Four Domains of Language

Although the four domains are not strategies, instruction for ELLs should involve as many of the domains of language as possible or appropriate to the lesson. These domains do not necessarily follow any particular progression or order when it comes to their development. Although speaking may not be dominant in the early stages, students will certainly be experimenting with the language, even if they do not feel ready or comfortable using it in the classroom. So although we do not want to force a level 1 or 2 student to speak before he or she is ready, we can engage them in highly active total physical response instruction that is appropriate for these early levels of language acquisition and will ultimately result in the development of all four domains of language.

Once students reach level 3 and above, all four domains can and should be activated during instruction. Here are some reminders about integrating the language domains:

- Reading, writing, listening, and speaking are naturally interrelated and integrated. We read when we write, and we listen when we speak to each other.

- Practice in any one of the four domains will result in improvement in the other three.

- By the time young children begin kindergarten at the age of five, they have generally become grammatically competent in their primary language. Thus, the holistic development of the four language domains makes more sense cognitively than developing them in isolation of each other, particularly because they are not acquired independently of each other.

- Connecting abstract and concrete concepts is best accomplished when students can incorporate and use all four language domains to practice and apply the new learning.

The following scenario looks at a classroom that incorporates listening, speaking, reading, and writing.

A Level 3 Science Lesson

Students will next be learning about space in their fourth-grade science class, so Ms. Prifti decides to begin by eliciting from students any prior knowledge they may have. She uses key vocabulary prediction, a strategy in which she asks students to think about space and then work with a partner to list all the words they think they will encounter when they read the next chapter of their science book. This helps her determine the level of prior knowledge her students have before she proceeds with the lesson.

Ms. Prifti sets the timer for three minutes, and students begin brainstorming and writing their words down. By the time the teacher calls time, each pair of students has a short list of words to share. She then gives the students a minute to practice reading their list of words to each other.

Now the students are ready to share out loud. Ms. Prifti goes around the room asking volunteers to share a word they think they might find in the next chapter, on space. By the end of the brainstorming session, she has listed the following words on a chart:

planet

moon

star

sun

cloud

spaceship

Based on the results of the brainstorm activity, Ms. Prifti decides it would be helpful to build some additional background knowledge because she suspects that the students have limited prior knowledge about space. She also notices that the word *cloud* is on the list, which could be evidence of some misconceptions.

In preparation for this possibility, she has previously taken short passages about space from lower-readability books, typed them onto strips of paper, and cut them out. She gives each student a strip, which she puts face down on their desks. On her signal, the students are to turn their strips over and read them, get up from their desk and walk around the room, meet a friend, read their passage to the friend, and then listen to the friend's passage. At the conclusion of this activity, students take out their science journals and write a prediction of the words about space they will encounter in the next chapter based on what they just heard from their friends.

Ms. Prifti asks the students to read the words they have predicted to their partners. Students are encouraged to share their own predictions or a partner's.

She concludes the lesson by asking students to help her add any new vocabulary to their class vocabulary prediction chart.

 ## Questions to Consider

1. Was this lesson appropriate for level 3 (speech emergence)?

2. How many opportunities did students have to:

    Listen?

    Speak?

    Read?

    Write?

3. How does having students actively using the four domains help increase their knowledge of the content?

4. Does your classroom incorporate a variety of listening, speaking, reading, and writing activities during practice and application? If not, what are some ways that you can ensure that you are providing many opportunities for students to engage in the four domains?

The Fifth Domain: Thinking

A wonderfully brilliant colleague of mine illuminated my thinking about the significance of critical thinking within the process of acquiring language for ELLs. Although thinking is not a language domain, it does play an important role in learning and acquiring language.

Many of us mistakenly believe that beginning-level ELLs have such limited English skills that deep critical thinking cannot be required of them or accessed. This is an erroneous notion, with the result that ELLs, particularly those in the preproduction and early production levels, are not being adequately challenged. This lack of rigorous instructional expectations may lead to high levels of disengagement.

There is another surprising connection between critical thinking and two of the other domains of language: reading and writing. Because reading and writing are constructive processes and the outcome of both processes is to construct meaning, both are considered highly cognitive in nature.[1] Due to the high levels of cognition involved in constructing meaning, research has shown that students become better critical thinkers when reading and writing are taught together. Chapters Twenty and Twenty-One highlight strategies that help to lead to improved critical thinking, the most effective being those that promote individual, personal responses to literature.[2]

Chapter 15

Making Content Comprehensible

In This Chapter

- Review of input theory
- Dissenting opinions about input theory
- Ideas for making content comprehensible

Stephen Krashen's input theory posits that successful acquisition of new knowledge occurs by simply understanding input that is a little beyond the learner's current level of understanding.[1] He defines that current level as i and the ideal level of new material as $i + 1$. In explaining the development of oral fluency, he theorizes that students figure out the meaning of words and grammar that are new to them through the use of context rather than direct instruction. Krashen has several areas he draws on for proof of his input hypothesis. He illustrates how good teachers tune their speech to their students' level, and how when talking to each other, second language learners adjust their speech in order to communicate. Comprehensible input, or $i + 1$, lies perfectly within the learner's zone

Ideas

- As with the implementation of all other strategies, make sure you always have the most recent data on language acquisition levels of your students. See the English Language Learner Profile Sheet in the Part Two Resources section.

- After identifying the topic, concepts, and skills you will be teaching, think about ways to make the content comprehensible to ELLs. Some ideas include using gestures, drawings, actions, facial expressions, variety in speech patterns, photographs, and objects to provide clues to meaning. Adding visual and kinesthetic support along with the language provides additional comprehensible input. The selection of approaches is dependent on the levels of ELLs in your class. For example, if you have no level 1 or 2 students, you may not need to provide so many gestures and facial expressions. However, you would still want to be sure that you used visuals and models to ensure that all students are fully grasping the content.

- If you are a mainstream teacher and have levels 1 and 2 students in your classroom, contact textbook publishers and inquire about primary language support materials. Although most offer direct translations to Spanish and some of the most common Asian languages, often support for other languages may be in the form of Web resources that students would have to link to from home. Keep in mind that not all students have access to technology at home. They can, however, go to a local library or use the materials while in class.

- If you are able to acquire textbook materials in students' primary language, levels 1 and 2 students should not work on these alone. They should be actively engaged in learning. The chapters in Part Five set out reading and comprehension strategies that highly engage ELLs.

of proximal development, the ideal level at which a student can successfully acquire new learning.

Judie Haynes encourages ESL and bilingual teachers to help mainstream teachers and their students communicate with new non-English-speaking students from the day these students arrive by providing comprehensible input to ensure that students feel welcome.[2]

This is particularly important if no or only a few adults at the school speak the language of a new student. You can encourage this interaction to take place by having a group of students who speak the different primary languages represented in your school be partnered with newcomers. These students can help orient the newcomers to the school. Although they cannot provide constant second-language translation during classroom instruction, they can step in to help the newcomer when the teacher simply cannot get an idea across to the new student.

Krashen reminds us that when planning instruction for ELLs, "The best methods are therefore those that supply 'comprehensible input' in low anxiety situations, containing messages that students really want to hear. These methods do not force early production in the second language, but allow students to produce when they are 'ready', recognizing that improvement comes from supplying communicative and comprehensible input, and not from forcing and correcting production."[3]

This theory does have many critics, mostly disagreeing with Krashen's idea that direct instruction in such matters as grammar need not be extensive because most language structures can be learned or picked up in context. There is also some disagreement among researchers as to whether all that it takes to move students to proficiency is comprehensible input. Some educators believe that this theory promotes the idea that students play a passive role in their language development. They believe instead that the effort students make in attempting to understand input, not simple comprehension, fuels acquisition of new knowledge.[4]

I do not recommend one approach over another, and leave it to teachers to decide which ones work best with their students. As with all other things, balance should be the prevailing constant in the application of any theories and approaches.

Chapter 16

Total Physical Response

In This Chapter

- Total physical response (TPR) defined

- What TPR is not

- The progression of TPR

The research base for total physical response (TPR) dates back to the 1960s. In an effort to help control seizures in patients with epilepsy, experiments were performed with epileptic volunteers whose right and left brain hemispheres had been surgically severed. The theory was that since seizures begin on one side of the brain and slowly move to the other side, isolating the seizure to one side of the brain could lessen the intensity of the event. After surgery, the volunteers underwent a large number of tests that began to reveal the different functions of the right and left hemispheres, and chief among them were language and movement.[1]

Among the researchers studying the different functions of the brain and the impact of this procedure was James J. Asher, psychologist and author of *The Total Physical Response Approach*.[2] Through these studies, he began to investigate some interesting relationships between language and movement, and this work led him to formulate the theory known today as TPR. The basic premise behind TPR is that language is acquired in the same way that it has been throughout recorded history. Parents speak continuously to their children, modeling actions and not expecting language production in return until the child is ready. For example, the parent talks through actions such as "Look at mama. Good, you're looking at mama!" or "Bring me your teddy bear. Good job!" And so it progresses, with production of the language lagging far behind comprehension often by years. For school-age children and adults, the progression is much more rapid than it is for toddlers because their range and ability for physical response is vast when compared with younger children. Therefore, language production begins to happen naturally, with students not even being aware that they are producing language.

This relationship between language and movement has been generalized to working with learners of any language. Asher believes that its success can be attributed to three factors:

- It is aptitude free, meaning that children and adults of any level can learn a language through TPR.

- It has been shown to work by study after study with adults and children all over the world.

- It is stress free because it does not require or demand the production of language.

TPR is also highly motivating because the levels of retention are high. For this reason, it proves to be highly motivational to both students and teachers alike.

My experience with TPR has led me to believe that there is much confusion about what it means. I have had teachers tell me that TPR simply means using physical movements while teaching. Although physical motion is in fact part of TPR, it is much more, and it is important that teachers know exactly what it encompasses in order to use it fully.

Asher recommends beginning TPR by reviewing the relevant textbook and listing all adjectives, adverbs, verbs, and nouns that can be internalized using TPR. For example, before starting a chapter on oceans in science, the teachers would review the instructional materials and develop a list of words, such as *wave, fish, tides, ashore,* and *fishing*. Once this information has been gathered, teachers who work with levels 1 and 2 students in particular can begin implementing TPR in their classrooms. The following scenario sets out a progression that might take place during structured ESL time. Notice how the instruction mostly is about basic survival vocabulary.

Using TPR in Level 1

Initially Mr. Winn calls out commands (for example, "Stand," "Sit," "Walk," "Run," "Turn," and "Jump") and then does the action as students watch him. After some time, his students become involved in the process by mimicking his physical motions. Students do not repeat the words until they are ready to produce language.

The next day, Mr. Winn continues by stringing a few words together—for example, "Stand and turn around," "Walk to the table," "Walk to the door," and "Walk to my desk." He presents these all one at a time until he thinks students are ready to attempt more than one action at a time. He will then say, for example, "Luz, stand up and walk to the table." The student will follow the teacher's multiple commands, and other students will follow Luz.

After several days of practicing these commands, students have the opportunity to play the role of the teacher and to call out commands. They have had plenty of opportunities to practice by this point, so they will feel confident. Even level 1 students will not feel anxious participating because they have been well supported and feel that they have been set up for success.

It's always important not to force a student to speak if he or she is not ready. Remember that the highest levels of learning take place in a safe environment that lowers the affective filter.[3]

Ultimately TPR equips ELLs at the earliest levels of language acquisition to experience comprehension and production in the target language without stress or anxiety. Besides Asher's opinions as to the reasons TPR is so successful, we also know that "acquisition requires meaningful interaction in the target language—natural communication—in which speakers are concerned not with the form of their utterances but with the messages they are conveying and understanding."[4]

Other teachers can use similar strategies as those in the scenario, although with differentiation for students of higher levels of language acquisition. In those classrooms, the teachers can use TPR to teach grammar or vocabulary. For example, if the lesson in a level 3 class is teaching possessives, you can use commands such as "Maria, give Jairo's book to Mohammed." "Qyuen, touch Maria's pencil." After the teacher uses these commands, students take over, modeling the possessive form while calling out commands to their classmates.

Chapter 17

Sheltered Instruction

In This Chapter

- Sheltered instruction defined
- Examples of sheltered instruction
- Examples of sheltered instructional strategies

Sheltered instruction is a set of strategies for teaching content to English language learners in strategic ways that make the subject matter concepts comprehensible while simultaneously promoting the students' English language development.[1] They reflect Stephen Krashen's input theories and are built on the premise of making content comprehensible as well as parallel to the content that mainstream students receive.

Sheltered instruction came about as a way of ensuring equal access to content. While "equal access" to some may mean that all students receive the same instruction, ELLs in fact need their instruction to look different. Sheltered instruction is designed for nonnative speakers who have reached an intermediate level of English proficiency and a functional level of language acquisition. These are students who need to develop cognitive academic language proficiency. Sheltered instruction structures learning activities in a way that helps build academic language. It is not watered-down curriculum; in fact, it is based on grade-level content.

Although sheltered instruction was designed for students who have reached intermediate fluency, these strategies are considered effective to use with all students. They incorporate higher-order thinking, schema theory, collaborative and cooperative learning, and writing. In order to achieve its purpose of access to content, teachers use such aids as visuals, objects, artifacts, pictures, models, graphs, and charts.

Examples of Sheltered Instruction

Many strategies are part of a sheltered instruction program, and a number of them are featured in the chapters in Part Five. But three of them define the essence of what sheltered instruction should look like in action.

Graphic Organizers and Concept Maps

Graphic organizers and concept maps play a large role in the sheltered classroom because they help students organize and store new information as well as connect new knowledge to existing knowledge. They also help students see the relationship among often disparate-looking pieces of knowledge. Ultimately graphic organizers help students focus their attention on the most important details. Among the many graphic organizers are these:

- *Comparison-and-contrast matrix.* Students determine similarities and differences between two historical events, people, characters, things, solutions, organisms, stories, ideas, or cultures.

- *Flowcharts.* These illustrate sequential events, decision-making process, assignment completion, and study skills.

- *Matrix diagrams.* These encompass schedules, statistics, problem solving, and comparisons with multiple criteria.

- *Fishbone diagrams.* These can be used to show cause-and-effect or a time line.

In the early stages of instruction, the teacher and students complete graphic organizers collaboratively, with the teacher modeling the thought processes that go into organizing the information in a way that makes sense. Once students have completed a number of graphic organizers with different topics, they are slowly transitioned from whole group to partners, then eventually to filling them out independently.

Although graphic organizers are largely considered to be instruction tools, they can be used effectively as an assessment for ELLs whereby the completed graphic organizer provides evidence of a student's comprehension of a topic.

Schema Building

In schema building, teachers help students make explicit connections to previous learning. We know from research that the richer the schema (prior knowledge) is for a given topic, the better the student will comprehend the topic. Teachers tap prior knowledge in an effort to access what students bring with them that they may be able to connect to the new learning. When prior knowledge is limited, as in the science lesson presented in Chapter Fourteen, the teacher works to build background, thereby facilitating the connection to new learning. Teachers understand that a schema is what students bring with them, and every student's schema is different. Therefore, tapping prior knowledge and building background knowledge become critical to students who are connecting with new learning.

Word Study

Word study is another sheltered strategy for teaching content from math to history. By studying the Greek and Latin origins of words, as well as prefixes, suffixes, and syllables, ELLs begin to see connections and patterns in the language around them. They can, for example, connect the prefix *tri-* with the number 3, which helps them remember that a triangle has three angles. Identifying Latin and Greek word sources also helps make the connection between spelling and vocabulary explicit. To continue with the example, understanding the vocabulary behind each part of the word *tri-angle* helps a student solidify the meaning of the word and reinforces the spelling.

Word study is particularly helpful to students whose language derives from Greek or Latin, and that around prefixes, suffixes, and syllables is beneficial to all students.

Sheltered Instruction Strategies

The following list provides some high-impact strategies that can be easily integrated into any lesson:[2]

- Use student-friendly language to communicate language and content objectives.

- Activate and use students' prior knowledge to connect new learning with their prior experiences.

- Build background knowledge for students who may lack prior knowledge about the content being taught.

- Use visuals, realia, manipulatives, graphic organizers, models, technology, and other resources to help explain concepts.

- Modify speech appropriately. For example, use slower speech, and control your use of slang and idioms.

- Use body language, gestures, mime, and acting to build meaning.

- Establish a positive affective environment by acknowledging and respecting cultural and linguistic diversity.

- Negotiate and clarify meaning throughout each lesson.

- Use appropriate questioning techniques such as wait time and periodic comprehension checks.

Conclusion

According to the Education Alliance, the success of sheltered English instruction depends on two integrated factors.[3] First, the teacher must be adept at providing modified instruction in English without watering down or oversimplifying the content. This is essential because all students, including ELLs, need to achieve mastery of the content. Second, to avoid what some refer to as fossilization of language skills at the social or conversational level, the teacher must engage students in a way that helps them with academic language. The challenge for teachers is simplifying their discourse, rather than the content, to make content comprehensible and then gradually make their language more complex without sacrificing the quality of instruction or depth of comprehension of the content.

Chapter 18

English as a Second Language

The need for English as a Second Language (ESL) programs to help U.S. students achieve language proficiency in English is evident from the results of the 2000 Census, which found that close to one in five U.S. citizens spoke a language other than English at home. The census also found that roughly 10 percent spoke English either less than fluently or not at all. ESL is designed for students whose primary language is not English. ESL programs can accommodate students from different language backgrounds in the same class, and teachers do not need to be proficient in the home languages of their students.

The purpose of ESL programs is to provide instruction for English learners on the structures, forms, and patterns of the English language. ESL should be thought of as a content area in its own right, with its own standards, textbooks, and materials.[1] By contrast, *sheltered instruction* refers to strategies that can be used to teach any content area, including ESL.

According to Spillett, ESL instruction should focus on four skill areas:[2]

1. *The function of language.* The purpose of language is communication, which encompasses social conversation, asking questions, and communicating ideas.

2. *The form of language. Form* refers to the structure of the English language, such as its grammar, sentence structure, and syntax. The form of the language represents its building blocks.

3. *Fluency. Fluency* refers to the ease with which we speak a particular language. It takes an ample amount of time dedicated to learning English in order to become fluent. Although ESL usually focuses on speaking, *fluency* can also refer to reading.

4. *Vocabulary.* In order to become proficient, ELLs must develop a broad and varied vocabulary. Research shows that they should be taught the key vocabulary associated with a topic, referred to as *brick words,* prior to a lesson in order to assist them in their language development. This means that before each lesson, students are taught the vocabulary they will encounter in that lesson in an effort to build their background knowledge and ensure they are receiving comprehensible input when they are taught the lesson. Another significant feature of ESL is providing comprehensible input in the form of visuals, gestures, and objects.

How English Learners Are Placed in ESL Classes

All English learners are required to be assessed every year in their progress in acquiring English. They are assessed in all four domains: listening, speaking, reading, and writing. Using the results of their state's English language proficiency assessment, schools typically group students by overall language proficiency levels, although some districts focus solely on the listening and speaking scores for placement at the appropriate level. Most teachers use the results of such assessments to help them form an accurate picture of each student's proficiency, as well as his or her specific needs.

Regardless of the method used, it is essential for schools and districts to have a consistent set of criteria for placing students appropriately. Placing students in the wrong ESL class can have devastating repercussions, particularly if these groupings stay constant through the course of an entire year. For example, a student who was initially assessed at level 2 and has progressed to level 3 yet remains in the same group will spend the entire school year receiving instruction that is unaligned with his or her proficiency. Students in this situation may find ESL classes boring or unchallenging, and they may become discouraged and disengaged. The chapters in Part Two offered ideas and solutions for preventing this from happening, including developing your own language acquisition assessment that can be administered throughout the year. Its results can then be used to place students in the appropriate level of ESL.

 Questions to Consider

1. Does the child have support at home for learning English—for example, older or younger siblings in the house with whom he or she can practice English?

2. Did the student attend school in his or her native country? If so, to what grade level?

3. What are the student's language and literacy levels in his or her primary language? In English?

4. Are other content-area teachers knowledgeable about strategies to use with English learners? Will English learners receive adequate support during content-area instruction?

5. Do other content teachers know the language acquisition levels of their English learners?

6. Do other content-area teachers understand second language acquisition?

The responses to questions 1 to 3 will help your school or district gather the necessary background information about your English learners, which will help in designing an ESL program that takes into consideration the needs of English learner population. The responses will also help your school or district ensure that content-area teachers are equipped with the appropriate knowledge and skills to successfully teach their content to English learners.

Once you've ensured proper placement of ELLs, the next challenge is developing high-quality ESL instruction that reflects both language and content goals.

ESL Programs

The content for ESL is defined by each state's language proficiency standards, but the nuances of the program depend on other factors. For example, your school site might offer a late-exit bilingual program in which students receive primary language instruction and gradually increase the amount of English they are taught over the course of five to seven years. In this case, ESL plays a vital role in teaching English structures and patterns and may even teach content vocabulary in the weeks leading up to lessons on that content.

If instead your school site offers only English mainstream classes for ELLs, then ESL will need to help fill in all of the content gaps that students may have from being immersed in English with little support. In this situation, it is essential for ESL teachers to work collaboratively and support each other in planning appropriate lessons for English learners.

ESL classes at the elementary level focus primarily on teaching the English alphabet and phonetics through a combination of strategies, including visual and hands-on strategies that are highly engaging. ESL at the secondary level consists of a class period devoted to ESL. English learners are sometimes required to take ESL as an exploratory course in, say, band, woodshop, or photography, which means that they are not getting access to these other areas of interests. Schools using this system need to consider whether this is the best option for their English learners and whether they believe it is equitable for English learners to not have an opportunity to take an exploratory class.

ESL Curriculum Materials

Although ESL curriculum may vary from state to state, all states are required by No Child Left Behind to provide ESL instructional programs. The problem with most textbooks is that they are not sufficiently challenging for English learners who are at level 3 or above. This presents a serious challenge for teachers who are often left to develop their own ESL program since the materials they have seem inadequate.

If your school or district has a pattern of students who get to level 3 in their language acquisition and are not reclassified, it is time to look at the level of instruction these students are receiving.

 Questions to Consider

- How many ELLs in third grade and above have not progressed from level 3 in over a year?

- At the secondary level, how many level 3 students have been at that level for a considerable amount of time?

- What program or materials are we using to teach ESL to students at level 3 and above?

- Are our level 3 ELLs reaching proficiency in English language arts and math? To find out, examine local and state assessment results over the course of at least three years, paying particular attention to the achievement of level 3 ELLs.

English as a Second Language is no doubt an integral part of every ELL's development of proficiency in English. We also must ensure that ESL programs are not insular. We cannot afford to have ESL teachers working in isolation of the mainstream education or sheltered instruction teachers. Instead they must work in concert with all mainstream education teachers to ensure that the general education teachers are providing appropriate instruction for ELLs outside the ESL block. The English Language Learner Profile Sheet in the Part Two Resources section can help provide mainstream teachers with critical information about their English learners.

The Questions to Consider in this section should be used as a way to begin a conversation about equity for English language learners. It is especially crucial for all educators to clearly understand that "equal treatment" does not necessarily result in equity.

English language learners do not require equal instruction to what native speakers receive. In fact, the equitable classroom instruction provided to them may look quite different from what is provided for native English speakers. For example, they may require textbooks in their primary language, opportunities to work cooperatively, primary language support from other students in the classroom, and other strategies that help them access the content. Nevertheless, in spite of these differences, all students should have the same instructional outcome.

Content-Based Instruction for ESL

Content-based ESL programs encompass structured immersion and sheltered English. All of these programs share the goal of teaching English language learners both English language and academic content simultaneously. In other words, teachers use the content to teach language objectives. They use a variety of strategies, such as gestures, visual aids, and simplified English, so that students can access content.

Content-area learning becomes increasingly difficult as students progress through each grade level. By the time students reach fifth grade and have transitioned from learning to read to reading to learn, textbooks and materials have become more challenging to access. Content-based ESL provides a time during the day when ELLs are placed in content classes by level and teachers use content as a vehicle for teaching the form and function of the English language.

When it comes to accessing content, here are some specific challenges that ELLs face when reading content material in English:[3]

- An increase in the amount of content-specific vocabulary

- Complex sentence structure and syntax

- Difficulty reading and understanding informational text

- Difficulty understanding what the teacher says

- Use of higher-level thinking skills in reading and writing

- Large amounts of text and information covered, with ELLs often not sure of what is important information and what is not

- Visuals that may be unclear, confusing, or difficult to understand

We next look at two models of content-based instruction for ELLs: content-driven ESL and content-based ESL.

Content-Driven ESL

In this model, ESL teachers "front-load" academic learning before it takes place during the mainstream class. This means that at least a few weeks before a particular topic is taught, the mainstream teachers have met with the content-area teachers to identify the essential vocabulary, language, and text structures that students may encounter in the textbooks. The ESL teacher uses the ESL block to build background knowledge that will help students be successful during the regular content instruction.

This model can make an incredible difference in the ability of ELLs to access content. In order for this model to work, ESL teachers must work collaboratively with content-area teachers.

Content-Based ESL

In this model, teachers teach ESL through the content to learners who are enrolled in combination ESL and content classes according to their level of language acquisition. These students are typically not enrolled in a separate ESL class.

This model is difficult to monitor and maintain because often teachers depend on the content too heavily and fail to provide sufficient instruction in the structures and patterns of the English language, which is what ESL content should provide. In order for this model to be effective, teachers need to have language objectives as well as content objectives so that students learn language objectives within the context of a content area.

Although this model is not easy to implement, if it is the only option available in the school, then teachers must receive appropriate professional development so that they can plan language-objective-driven lessons. The Part Four Resources section contains a questionnaire for assessing ESL program effectiveness.

Part Four Resources

Assessing the Effectiveness of Our ESL Program

Rate each item from 1 to 5, with 1 being low implementation and 5 being high implementation. Use the results of this survey to begin assessing the effectiveness of your ESL program:

1. How well does our ESL program address the four skill areas?

   Function of language
   1   2   3   4   5
   Form of language
   1   2   3   4   5
   Fluency of language
   1   2   3   4   5
   Vocabulary
   1   2   3   4   5

2. How effectively do we place students in leveled ESL classes?

   1   2   3   4   5

3. How responsive is our ESL program when a student's language acquisition level changes?

   1   2   3   4   5

Part Five

Teaching Strategies Across the Content Areas

Part Five pulls together many of the elements from previous chapters, such as identifying language proficiency levels and making content comprehensible. It explores how to adapt high-impact, research-based strategies to meet the needs of English learners. The ultimate goal is the achievement of English language learners in both the core content and language acquisition. The chapters in this part focus on differentiating strategies so that language learners of all levels can acquire language and access content.

Chapter 19

High-Impact Strategies for Teaching the Content Areas

In This Chapter

- High-impact strategies for ELLs

- Effect size defined

The chapters in Part Five use research by John Hattie and Robert Marzano to identify some high-impact strategies that are appropriate for English learners and explains how to apply them in different content areas.[1] I have modified these strategies to include opportunities for students to actively engage the four domains of language—listening, speaking, reading, and writing—as well as the fifth domain, thinking. All strategies are coded with the following letters so that you can see at a glance what domains each one emphasizes:

L	Listening
S	Speaking
R	Reading
W	Writing
T	Thinking

Of course, the strategies that follow are not the only research-based ones that can be used with ELLs. In fact, any strategy can be used as long as it is appropriately differentiated to meet the needs of English learners at different levels of language acquisition.

In selecting strategies to highlight in the following chapters, I gave consideration to their appropriateness for English learners, as well as their overall impact on achievement as measured by effect size, that is, the strength of the relationship between two variables. Hattie has provided this explanation of how effect size translates into increased learning and achievement in the classroom: "An effect size of $d = 1.0$ indicates an increase of one standard deviation.... A one standard deviation increase is typically associated with advancing children's achievement by two to three years.... An effect size of 1.0 would mean that, on average, students receiving the treatment would exceed 84% of students not receiving the treatment."[2] Here are a few examples of strategies that you will encounter in the following chapters and their effect sizes:

Concept mapping, $d = 0.57$

Questions, $d = 0.93$

Note taking, $d = 0.99$

Reciprocal teaching, $d = 0.74$

Direct instruction, $d = 0.59$[3]

I recommend that you use the research to identify the most effective strategies and then plan your instruction and differentiation accordingly.

Chapter 20

Strategies for Reading

Because of its cognitive demands and dependence on language, reading can be one of the biggest challenges that English learners face. A major cause of this difficulty is the English learner's lack of academic vocabulary. However, we also know that along with limited vocabulary comes a lack of understanding of abstract concepts such as freedom or justice, which they are bound to encounter in content-area textbooks.[1] In fact, according to the American Federation of Teachers, the rate of reading failure for African American, Hispanic, limited-English-proficient, and low-socioeconomic-status children ranges from 60 to 70 percent.[2] The complexity of academic English is also an obstacle as English learners struggle to develop higher-level reading and writing skills.[3] Some studies have shown that

ELLs require as many as six to ten years to reach grade-appropriate proficiency in reading and writing in English.[4] Because reading is the fundamental skill on which all formal education depends, ensuring that ELLs develop effective comprehension skills becomes an essential priority, regardless of grade level.

After identifying levels of our English learners' English language proficiency, it is important to give special consideration to the best ways to teach and help them achieve. Knowing as much as we can about our students, their interests, and the ways they learn best are also critical factors in the selection of strategies and planning of instruction (see the student interest surveys in the Part Five Resources section).

There is no question that instincts and judgment play a significant role in teachers' instructional decisions, but research has shown that they're not enough. With the advent of standards and accountability has come a shift toward using data and research as the basis for instructional decisions versus relying solely on instincts and professional judgment.

Approaches to Reading for Elementary and Secondary English Learners

In the elementary grades, ELLs typically enter schools with little or no instruction in another language or education system. Because proficiency in the native language is one of the strongest predictors for success in acquiring a second language, the ideal setting for these students is a bilingual classroom in which reading is taught within the context of the primary language.[5]

Unfortunately, it is not always possible to provide a bilingual classroom for all English learners, particularly in a school with a diverse English learner population with many languages represented and few resources to meet their primary language needs. Nevertheless, whatever the situation, English learners in the elementary grades require high levels of support when it comes to reading instruction. The ESL class plays an integral role in front-loading vocabulary and providing extended opportunities for students to connect to and interact with text.

In contrast, instruction in the secondary grades is based on the assumption that students already have basic reading and writing skills and elementary content-area foundations. This assumption, however, is not always accurate. A high number of ELLs are entering secondary school with increasing levels of diversity, particularly with regard to their prior educational backgrounds. Kinsella, Stump, and Feldman write that with regard to prior schooling, ELLs at the secondary level tend to fall into one of the following broad but overlapping groups:[6]

1. Recent adolescent immigrants who have received a strong educational background in their native countries prior to immigration to the United States and are prepared with strong academic and study skills to apply to new subject matter

2. Language-minority students who attended U.S. elementary schools and are continuing into secondary schools with inadequate English fluency and literacy to compete in challenging academic content areas

3. Immigrant, refugee, and migrant students who have experienced little to no prior schooling and enter secondary school lacking basic literacy and elementary content-area foundations

Each of these groups has unique needs that cannot be met through a one-size-fits-all model. Addressing the needs of this diverse population requires taking a look at each individual student and planning instruction accordingly. Once we understand the strengths and obstacles they face, we can plan differentiated instruction that includes the use of research-based strategies, critical thinking, and the four language domains of reading, writing, speaking, and listening. As in the primary grades, secondary ESL classes need to identify the specific needs and backgrounds of the ELL population and then provide reading support taking those needs into account.

Whether we are working with elementary or secondary English learners, our ultimate goal is to provide strategies for students to use in order to understand the texts they read. Even beginning-level English learners can use strategies to comprehend text when teachers use books and realia that provide comprehensible input, choose topics that students can relate to their background experiences, create a low-anxiety environment, and encourage students to respond physically as well as verbally. These strategies set the foundation for English learners at all levels to be able to make connections to text, question, visualize, predict, and infer when reading.

Assessing Preexisting Reading Ability

Assessment of a student's current knowledge provides teachers with a starting point for instruction. Hattie writes that while feedback to students is critical, the feedback that teachers receive about what students can and cannot do is more powerful.[7] It stands to reason, then, that assessing a student's reading ability is a critical first step. Prior to beginning instruction, elementary English learners should be assessed in these key areas:[8]

- Phonemic awareness
- Letter knowledge
- Reading words
- Oral fluency

This initial assessment provides diagnostic information regarding any areas of weakness for ELLs. When English learners initially enroll in U.S. schools, their reading ability is typically assessed in their primary language. Their reading skills in English should be assessed as well. In their 2007 report on effective literacy instruction for English learners in the elementary grades, Gersten et al. listed screening for reading problems and monitoring progress as their first recommendation. They suggested that districts use the same measures and assessment approaches that are used with native English speakers to ensure that any English learner with reading problems is identified as early as possible so that they can receive structured and targeted intervention.[9]

For secondary English learners, reading assessment should include these areas:[10]

- Reading words
- Passage comprehension with retelling
- Fluency
- Accuracy

Language arts, content area, and ESL teachers can combine or cross-reference these results with results from the most recent English language proficiency assessment to help build a comprehensive reading profile that all teachers can use. If an assessment reveals that a secondary English learner has difficulties in reading that are not related to his or her English learner status, then additional screening should be done to determine specific areas of need.

Initial instruction for secondary ELLs typically begins with skill-building lessons that focus on decoding, word recognition, and pronunciation and then progressing to explicit instruction in comprehension strategies such as predicting, questioning, and summarizing that will help them deal more readily with the reading demands of content-area classrooms. This initial assessment assists teachers in determining the appropriate instructional starting point.

Comprehension: The Key to Accessing Content

Since reading is the gatekeeper to accessing all other content areas, we investigate the six elements important to reading comprehension: word recognition, the language of comprehension, text structure, comprehension strategies, motivation and attention, and background knowledge (Figure 20.1). In order for a student to interact with and comprehend text, all six elements must be present. All of these elements are discussed in this chapter except text structure, which is addressed in Chapter Twenty-Three, where the focus is on teaching English learners how to use the features of text to help aid comprehension.

The following sections discuss strategies that help build each of these elements of reading comprehension. It is important to note that although I have differentiated these strategies for English learners, they can be used with all learners.

Although comprehension of text presents teachers of English learners with significant challenges, there are concrete strategies we can use to increase a student's level

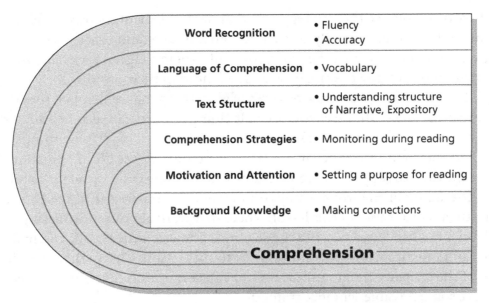

Figure 20.1 The Six Building Blocks of Comprehension

Source: Adapted from Reading Professional Development Institute (1999).

of comprehension. These strategies can be applied across content areas and can be differentiated according to students' needs.

Background Knowledge

Setting a purpose for reading can make the difference between a student who is highly motivated to read a text and a student who simply goes through the motions and does not comprehend. One of the best ways to set the purpose is to build background knowledge so that students' interest is piqued and so that they connect with what they are about to read.

Many teachers of English learners find that activating prior knowledge becomes a frustrating effort because so many of these learners have limited experiences. Although it is certainly true that many English learners lack the depth and quantity of life experiences that many native English speakers possess, there is no denying that all students have life experiences from which to pull in order to connect to new learning.

English learners, like all other students, require direct instruction in using a strategy before they can apply it fluently. Simply asking students to share their connections is not enough for them to learn how to apply a new strategy. Strategies should be modeled several times in order to help all students be successful.

The Strategy: Making Connections to Background Knowledge

It is important to choose text with topics that students, particularly English learners, will have had experience with, such as family, animals, pets, or moving.

The first time you use this strategy, whether at the elementary or secondary level, it is important to do it collaboratively so that students understand exactly what they will do. Clearly explain that as you read the story, you'd like them to listen for events in it that may remind them of something they may have experienced in their own lives.

Levels 1 and 2 students can draw pictures of something they remember; they do not need to write or speak unless they feel comfortable doing so. You can also use a handout with preprinted sentence frames, such as "I remember when . . ." or "This reminds me of . . ." and they add the connection they made. This is a temporary scaffold and should be used only when the time to copy the sentence frame will interfere with a student's ability to keep up with the reading of the story. A way to prepare these learners is to read a similar story during ESL class in advance of this lesson where they learn about remembering vocabulary.

For level 3 English learners, write the sentence frames on the board, and make sure you introduce and practice using the frames prior to this lesson. Clarify that they do not have to use all of the sentence frames unless they have a connection that goes with each frame.

Here are some possible sentence frames:

This part of the story reminds me of . . .

What I just read reminds me of . . .

This story makes me think about . . .

This reminds me of a time when . . .

I remember when . . .

The Strategy in Action: Domains L, S, W, and T

1. Make sure students have their reading journals open or sticky notes available to jot down their connections. You will also need chart paper to model the strategy. In the early elementary grades, students can share their connections orally.

2. Choosing a vivid text, picture book, or culturally relevant selection will help levels 1 and 2 students feel better able to connect with the story since they don't have to focus so much on language and instead can depend on photographs and drawings to help them connect to the story. Multiple readings are also essential to levels 1 and 2 English learners and will help build on the vocabulary they learned prior to this lesson during their ESL class. The preview during ESL class will also build their confidence, which will result in their active engagement with the text. In fact, this is ideally how ESL and the content areas can work in concert to ensure comprehensible input at all times. (See Chapter Fifteen for more information.)

3. As you read sections of the text, stop occasionally and make your own connections using think-alouds to talk through the specific memory, person, or event that you have connected with. It is important to model this sequence for students and teach

them that when they reach the end of a story, they should jot down whether they were reminded of a person, event, feeling, time, or place. They can then share their connection using the sentence frames.

4. Give students an opportunity to share their memories with a partner. Then ask if anyone would like to share a memory with the rest of the class. They can also share a memory they heard from a partner if the partner agrees this can be shared.

5. Jot down your own connections on chart paper using the sentence frames.

The Strategy: Making Connections—Text to Text, Text to Self, Text to World

Depending on the grade level and the English learner levels, you may want to practice the previous strategy several times with different books before moving on to this one, which takes the students' learning to the next level. Again, use a read-aloud of a story that students can connect to. Picture books provide lots of visual clues for English learners, who may depend on those clues for meaning.

Begin by defining three connections: text to text, text to self, and text to world:

- Text-to-text connections: those students make between events in the story and other books that they have read

- Text-to-self connections: those students make between events in the story and their own life experiences

- Text-to-world connections: those students make between events in the story and what is happening in the world

Students will have their journals open and will designate their connections as TT, TS, or TW.

The students will have had experience with text to self from the previous strategy, but may not be sure about text-to-text or text-to-world connections. In that case, think-alouds will play a major role in modeling for English learners how to make a text-to-text connection or what a text-to-world connection sounds like. Do not underestimate the value of using think-alouds particularly with ELLs at levels 1 and 2. Think-alouds provide a window into the reader's mind and helps teachers convey what effective readers do.[11]

The Strategy in Action: Domains L, S, R, W, and T

1. Read the story out loud. Then ask students to pay close attention to the events in the story and see if there are any connections they can make.

2. Now read the story again, this time modeling each of the three connections at least once. Again reinforce that after reading the story, the students should think about

connections they may have made, identify what the connection is, jot it down, and then share it with the class.

3. For English learners at levels 1 and 2 or in the early elementary grades, put the visuals on a poster that clearly shows and defines text to text, text to self, and text to world. The images will provide clues for the students about each of the different types of connections. (See Figure 20.2 for examples of these.)

4. At the conclusion of the second reading, students debrief with a shoulder partner by reviewing each of their connections and reading them to their partners. The debriefing process is essential because it provides an opportunity for students to learn about the world and each other, and perhaps gain further understanding of the text they read.

Once you feel confident in your students' ability to make connections with read-alouds, they can apply the same strategies to independent reading. They can collect their notes in their journals and share these connections as part of their independent reading reflections.

The Strategy: List-Group-Label

List-group-label is a brainstorming strategy that can be used prior to reading as a way of activating prior knowledge and then be revisited after reading as a way of adding to the knowledge that students previously had.[12] This strategy can be modified for use in grades K–12 and is an effective tool to use in activating all four domains of language as well as thinking.

The Strategy in Action: Domains L, S, R, W, and T

1. Students are given the topic of study and asked to brainstorm all the words they can associate with that topic. For example, if you are learning about oceans, ask students to list all the words they know that are associated with oceans. It is best to give students a minimum number of words to list.

2. Place students in groups of two to three and ask them to combine their individual lists into a group list and record that list on a group chart. As they compile their list, they are to look for or create categories that can encompass their words—for example, ocean animal life, ocean plant life, and oceans of the world. In deciding on categories and placing the individual words in the appropriate categories, students are activating and building background knowledge for the topic.

3. Equipped with this knowledge, students write predictions for what they expect to learn during the upcoming unit of instruction and add these predictions to their charts. The charts can be posted on the wall during the course of the unit and can act as a word wall that students can add to.

Text to Text

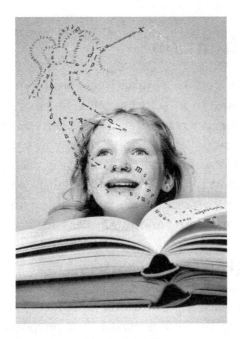

Text to Self

Text to World

Figure 20.2 Making Connections

4. Have students work in their groups to write questions for each of their categories. This will help focus and direct their learning during the unit of study. As they read the text and interact with the content, they should be alert to finding answers to their questions.

During the course of study, students add new information to their chart, including categories or facts that they learn about. By the end of the unit, each group's chart is rich with new learning. The completed charts serve as an ongoing assessment that helps you see the new information that students have acquired as a result of their learning.

Motivation and Attention

Teaching students strategies for connecting with text is an important first step in reframing the act of reading from a passive to an active process. For many students, reading becomes a pointless exercise because they are reading without a purpose and thus are not motivated to monitor their comprehension. These are precisely the students who will inform you that they have finished their reading, and yet when you ask them what they read about, the common response is "I don't know!" accompanied by a shrugging of the shoulders. This section provides strategies on how to use questioning and concept mapping to help students develop a purpose for reading and remain engaged throughout the reading.

The Strategy: Teaching Questioning

Just like making connections, asking questions is not a natural skill, especially when it comes to reading and helping the reader establish a purpose. Dole et al. write that the key to the effectiveness of the questions that students generate lies in the instruction they receive: students who received direct instruction on how to generate questions greatly outperformed students who were simply asked to generate questions and those who just reread the text.[13]

The Strategy in Action: Domains L and T

Begin by sharing your own questions about a text you are reading—a novel, short story, or informational text.

1. Photocopy one or two pages of the text, and project it using a document camera, SMART board, or overhead projector. Also have a number of markers of different colors on hand.

2. Begin reading the text out loud as students follow along with you. Stop at places where you have questions. Using the think-aloud strategy, talk through the question that occurred to you and use one color of marker to put a question mark

next to that portion of the text. An example of a question might be "Why did Anna [the main character] decide to leave? That's totally unexpected!"

3. Continue reading. If you come to the answer to your question, mark it in the margin with the same color marker that you used for the question.

4. Continue reading in this way, stopping to mark questions and answers, until you get to the end of the passage. Use a different color for each question–answer pair.

5. At the end of this collaborative modeling, show your students that some of the answers were right in the text. Others were not, but alert readers who were paying attention to details could surmise the answers. Also show the students that not all questions may have been answered.

6. Depending on the students, you may need to repeat this process. Another possibility is that a student could bring in a text that she or he was currently reading and use the modeled process to read through the passage with the class. Or you could model this with material the students were currently reading in class.

7. Students in upper grades could move on to categorizing types of questions, reading with the specific purpose of answering a question or reading with a specific question in mind.

The Strategy in Action: Domains L, S, and T

For students in K–3, you can move on to a second round of practice, the reading request method, which has three main parts.

1. Begin by reading a portion of the text, and then stop to ask questions. Be sure that your early questions are easy to answer. At this point, students don't answer the questions but rather listen carefully to how the questions are formed and asked. Thinking aloud is critical here so that students can pick up on the structure of the questions. You can also write down the questions and discuss the structure of the question; for example, "Is Mama's ring in the *maza*?" Don't take too much time on this, though; too much discussion of grammar can detract from comprehension.

2. Read another portion of the text, and this time ask one question only. Then ask the students if any of them can ask a question about the text. The sequence continues back and forth between teacher and students until the students have no more questions. The only rule is that a question must be fair, that is, the answer should be found in the text.

3. Before continuing to read, divide the room in half. A student from one side of the room will ask a question, followed by a student from the other side. This ends up being a game in which the objective is to see which side of the room asks the last fair question about the passage.

The purpose of these two strategies is to begin to teach students, particularly English learners who need help with the structure of the English language, how to ask questions. As you gradually modify these strategies, the students begin to independently practice the strategy during their own reading.

An opportunity for the application of this strategy can take place during independent reading. Students can use sticky notes with a question mark to show where they have a question and a sticky note with an A (for "answer") showing where in the text they discovered the answer to their question. After practicing this strategy over a short period of time, students will begin to understand that reading is an active process and that reading driven by questions is more engaging than reading without asking questions.

A way to keep track of the questions developed before, during, and after reading a text is to create a chart with three distinct sections:

- Our questions before we read the book:

- Our questions while we read the book:

- Our questions after we read the book:

Have students work with partners, writing their questions on sticky notes and then adding their stickies to a class chart. In this way, you create a model of how we should all be questioning at all times during the reading process—before, during, and after.

The Strategy: Teaching Students How to Predict

As with making connections and asking questions, prediction is a learned skill that requires direct instruction, particularly for English learners and students in elementary grades. By the time they've reached middle and high school, students typically have more experience with prediction and may not require much further instruction. Of course, we cannot afford to make assumptions with skills that are this important to comprehension. You will need to assess this skill at the secondary level to determine whether your students possess it. In fact, newcomers or English learners who arrived in U.S. schools in middle or high school with no previous schooling may not have developed this skill at all. Again, taking a close look at the needs of your students will determine whether and how you use this strategy.

Directed Listening Thinking Activity. The directed listening thinking activity (DLTA) applies to students who lack basic literacy skills:

The Strategy in Action: Domains L, S, and T

1. Read the title of the text to the students, and ask them to make predictions about what they think the story might be about based on just the title. Record on chart paper any predictions they offer.

2. Read another portion of the text and ask students to (1) check their previous predictions, (2) make new predictions based on the information they just received, and (3) revise any predictions they previously made that turned out not to be correct.

3. Continue this predict, confirm, and revise sequence in portions until you finish the story.

This DLTA strategy helps students who are not reading become actively engaged with a text. Once young children learn this skill, they can apply it to other materials that are read to them in class. By the time these children have developed their reading skills, they will have internalized this strategy and be able to apply it effortlessly.

Directed Reading Thinking Activity. The directed reading thinking activity (DRTA) follows the same exact sequence as DLTA except it uses text and reading skills rather than listening skills.

The Strategy in Action: Domains L, S, R, W, and T

1. Present students with the title of a story, and ask them to think about the story based on title: "What do you think will happen in the story? Why do you think that will happen?" Accept all answers with equal enthusiasm. However, if you find that your students' responses are too generic, then use the 5 W's (who, what, where, when, and why) to help them come up with more specific language and predictions— for example, "Mai, you said that the girl will be sad. Why do you think that?" Keep in mind that not all students, particularly those at levels 1 and 2, will make a prediction. You can still ask them yes-or-no questions appropriate to their understanding and language proficiency—for example, "Mai, is the girl sad?"

2. Now give the students the next part of the text to read. Make sure to specify to what page you'd like them to read. At that point, students are to decide if they want to keep their predictions or revise them. If students have arrived at a part that shows their prediction was right, they need to share not just that their prediction was correct, but where in the text they discovered that they were right. Thus, there can be two types of responses from this point on: their prediction was right, in which case they need to show where in the text they knew they were right, or the prediction was wrong, and they need to show where in the text they realized that. The most important part of this strategy is that students must not just state whether their predictions are correct but must also identify the part in the text that shows whether they were correct.

3. Continue the process, allowing students to read up to a certain page and come back to their predictions to decide whether they were correct, all the while backing their responses with evidence from the text.

You will notice that students get overly engaged in this process and may read ahead and not stay with the rest of the class. If that becomes an issue, you can project the story so that you can control how far they read each time.

At the conclusion of this process, lead a discussion that touches on important lessons or issues brought up in the story.

Higher-level thinking can be encouraged by reading this story a second time, paying attention to different details and nuances in the story that the students may not have picked up on originally. Whereas the first reading helps students discover the "within" story predictions, the second reading helps them identify "beyond" story issues. This is where lots of critical, high-level thinking takes place.

Differentiation for English Learners at Levels 1 to 3.   English learners who are level 1, level 2 , or even level 3 may struggle with writing down their predictions. For levels 1 and 2 students, who may not be fluent readers, keep in mind that the text may need to be read to them.

You can also encourage levels 1 to 3 English learners to draw or illustrate their predictions and then label them using a few words or phrases. They may also choose to role-play their predictions if that is more comfortable for them.

Remember to differentiate according to the students' strengths and needs. If, for example, you know that a few of your level 2 students are ready to write and prefer to do so, then don't require them to draw or illustrate the assignment.

The Strategy: Tea Party

In this prereading strategy, have students interact in an effort to have them share information with each other regarding the reading of an upcoming text. This strategy can be used with either narrative or expository text and helps students predict and establish a purpose for reading. The strategy in action examples involve using portions of text. In the early elementary grades, illustrations from the text can be used instead of sentence strips or passages.

We look at two variations of the tea party: (1) students interact with one or a few sentences at most (the sentence strip method) or (2) they interact with larger, paragraph portions of text (the passage method). Either method works well, so choose the variation based on the needs and levels of your students. The paragraphs may be more appropriate for a novel that students will read over an extended period of time, whereas the sentence strips are more appropriate for use with short stories or chapters of text.

Sentence Strip Method.
The Strategy in Action: Domains: L, S, R, W, and T

1. Pull sentence strips from a story that contain scenes, characters, or emotions that may be significant to the plot of the story. If you are using the strategy with

nonfiction text, you will need to be selective about the phrases you choose so that they provide enough context and information for the students to be able to make predictions. Run off enough sets of strips for each group or table in your room. Cut out the strips and put them into an envelope. You should have one envelope per group and one strip for each person in the group.

2. You are now ready for a tea party! Give each table an envelope with the strips inside. One person from each table passes out the strips to each person in the group. At your prompting, the students walk around the room connecting with a different person each time they stop and read their sentence or phrase to each other.

3. Call time when all students have had sufficient opportunity to share their sentence strips and gather information from other students.

4. Students return to their tables, sequence their sentence strips, and formulate a prediction based on what they heard and read while they were sharing. They can glue the strips onto poster paper or a large piece of construction paper and write their prediction along the bottom portion of the chart. The groups are then asked to share their predictions.

5. The next day, have the students read the text. The groups are allowed to revisit their predictions and revise them during the reading of the story. In the end, it is interesting to see which group got the closest in terms of predicting accurately.

Passage Method.

The Strategy in Action: Domains: L, S, R, W, and T

1. Select four different paragraphs or passages and photocopy them, along with a set of directions that ask the student to read through all four passages thoroughly. What students don't know is that although the direction sheet may look the same, the passages on the sheets are different. In fact, you should run off at least four different sets of passage sheets with directions printed on them so that each group has its own set of passages. In order for them to look uniform, so that the students are not aware of the differences, select paragraphs that are similar in length so that when the pages are run off, they look essentially the same. Provide each group with a piece of chart paper.

2. You are now ready for a tea party! Each individual receives a direction sheet that includes the extended passages. All students in one group should get the same four passages.

3. Students work at their tables and read the passages to each other. They then attempt to sequence them into the order that everyone agrees they go in. Everyone must be in agreement before the passages can be cut out and glued onto the chart

paper. After deciding on the sequence, cutting out the paragraphs, and gluing them on the chart paper, the students need to come up with a prediction of what they think this story or content that will be read will be about. They add the prediction to the bottom of their poster.

4. Once all groups of students have glued their paragraphs and come up with their predictions, open up the discussion to the whole class. Although all the passages come from the same text, the fact that they are different and possibly taken from different parts of the book will make for some interesting discussion. There may be some initial confusion when students realize each table has been working with different paragraphs; however, it will not distract from the liveliness of the discussion over the different predictions. It is also interesting to hear how the paragraphs were sequenced together.

5. The next day, have the students read the text. The groups are allowed to revisit their predictions and revise them during the reading of the story. In the end, it is interesting to see which group got the closest in terms of predicting accurately.

Comprehension Strategies

We are now ready to put the skills of making connections, asking questions, and making predictions to work within the context of reciprocal teaching, a reading comprehension strategy. These strategies help teach students how to read actively and monitor their reading.

The Strategy: Reciprocal Teaching

Reciprocal teaching, a strategic reading strategy, is a form of dialogue between the teacher and the students in which they take turns assuming the role of teacher and leading the discussion about a story or passage in the text.[14] It is a systematic strategy for teaching readers how to interact with and comprehend text. Reciprocal teaching can be used to engage readers with both narrative and expository text. As students become more confident in their abilities, they take on more leadership until they are facilitating the process themselves while the teacher simply monitors.[15]

Palincsar and Brown found that when reciprocal teaching was used for fifteen to twenty days, students' reading comprehension on assessments increased from 30 to 80 percent.[16] Later, Palincsar and Klenk found that students were able to maintain their improved comprehension skills up to a year later.[17] Hattie found that when reciprocal teaching was implemented fully, it had an effect size of 0.74.[18] (Remember from Chapter Nineteen that an effect size of this magnitude translates to students making two to three years of growth.) Reciprocal teaching has been found to be particularly beneficial for English learners because of its systematic teaching and practice of strategic reading strategies. It also provides English learners with the vocabulary of comprehension, such as predicting, questioning, summarizing, and clarifying.

Four strategies make up reciprocal teaching:

- *Prediction,* which activates prior knowledge about the text and helps readers make connections between new information and what they already know

- *Clarifying,* which promotes deep comprehension as students share their uncertainties about unfamiliar vocabulary, confusing text passages, and difficult concepts

- *Questioning* or *question generating,* which encourages readers to engage with the text rather than responding only to teacher questions

- *Summarizing,* which collaboratively enables all readers to increase comprehension of difficult texts

The teacher teaches and models all four of these strategies numerous times until the dialogue among students becomes natural and the groups are being run by students. The ultimate goal is for students to be able to use these strategies automatically as needed to gain comprehension.

The level and amount of teacher-directed experiences is determined by grade level, ELLs' language proficiency levels, and the content area. Once you fully understand the instructional sequence, you will be able to judge which of the two structures for implementation is more beneficial to your group of students: (1) follow the initial sequence as closely as possible or (2) begin by introducing and defining each of the four comprehension strategies of predicting, questioning, summarizing, and clarifying. Form 20.1 provides cards with information on each strategy and sentence starters. Run these cards off (enlarged) on tagboard, and laminate them if you plan to reuse them. Make sure that each child has a complete set of four cards.

Form 20.1 Reciprocal Teaching Student Cards

Card 1: Predicting

A good prediction is based on:

- What has already happened in the story
- An understanding of the type of story I'm reading
- The pictures, captions, and other text clues
- Facts and is not just a random guess

Prediction Sentence Frames

1. My prediction is_____. (K-1)
2. I predict that_____. (K-2)
3. If we look at the_____we can tell that_____. (3–12)
4. Now that I have scanned the text, I have come to the conclusion that_____. (3–12)
5. I hypothesize that_____.(3–12)
6. I bet that_____. (3–12)

Card 2: Questioning

Good questions are based on:

- Things you hope to learn about in the text
- Clues in the prereading activities
- Something you expect might be answered
- Patterns in the text that you think may continue

Question Sentence Frames

1. I want to know if_____.
2. I'm wondering if we will learn about_____ _____.
3. I have a question about_____.
4. I've always wondered if_____.
5. Who is_____?
6. Why did_____?
7. What would happen if_____?

Card 3: Clarifying

When you come to something you do not understand, do the following:

- Reread the sentence.
- Identify parts of the word that you know.
- Sound the word out. See if it make sense with the rest of the sentence.
- Substitute a word or idea that might make sense in its place.
- Identify which part of the story doesn't make sense.

Clarification Sentence Frames

1. What does the author mean by_____ _____?
2. I don't understand what it meant when_____ _____.
3. I need clarification on _____.
4. I agree with you. This means_____.
5. I do not agree with you. I think it means_____ _____.
6. This part is really saying _____.

Card 4: Summarizing

Good summaries always include:

- Key ideas and concepts
- Key words
- Key places
- Key people or items

Summary Sentence Frames

1. This story/paragraph is mainly about _____ _____.
2. The topic sentence is _____.
3. The author is trying to tell me _____ _____.
4. This is mostly about _____.
5. This chapter's main idea is_____ _____.

The Strategy in Action: Domains L, S, R, and T

1. Using either an easy narrative or expository text, begin by modeling the process. Students should have cards from Form 20.1 that define each of the four strategies and include sentence frames. Up through sixth grade, it would be helpful to post a chart with the sentence starters that students can refer to. Use a prereading strategy prior to going any further. Point out the titles, headings, and subheadings of the reading passage. That information will help both teacher and students make valid predictions.

2. Begin by making a prediction, such as "I predict that we will learn about Native American tribes of the Southwest." Students follow with their own predictions that you keep track of in order to confirm whether they are correct. For example, a student may add "I think I will learn about the homes they lived in." Continue in this way until you have a sufficient number of predictions and you see that students are ready to move on.

3. Now turn to questions. Using the think-aloud strategy, talk through your own questions and specifically the thinking that led you to the questions you've formulated. Record your questions, and ask for student volunteers to read their questions, which can be added to the chart paper. An example of a question would be "Will we learn about the types of food that Native Americans of the Southwest ate?"

4. The class is now ready to begin reading. Before they start, remind students that they should be looking for answers to their questions, evidence as to whether their prediction was accurate, and any questions or clarification they may have about the text. Depending on the grade and language learner levels, you may either have students read the section individually, in their groups, or the teacher may read the text aloud.

5. After they have completed the reading, ask about the predictions they made and whether they discovered evidence of being right or wrong. Model by reading the passages from the text that support your predictions.

6. Next, read the passages from the text that you labeled A because they answered your questions. Ask students to share whether they found the answers to their questions and, if so, where in the text they did so.

7. It makes sense to model clarifying here since students will likely encounter terminology relating to ideas that are unfamiliar while they read a text. Take a moment to ask a clarifying question so that you can model what they are supposed to sound like—for example, "I need clarification on what the word *prickly pear* means." See if anyone in the classroom can offer clarification. Allow other students the opportunity to ask their clarifying questions.

8. Finally, write a summary using the information you gathered from your prereading to provide the structure for your thoughts. Have a poster prepared in advance that includes titles, headings, and subheadings with blank spaces in between. Ask different students to volunteer summary statements and add them to the appropriate section of the poster. Remember to require students to use the appropriate vocabulary from their sentence frames when they volunteer to contribute to the class chart paper. At the end, you will have a summary that includes all of the ideas shared by your students.

Although this may sound like a complex process, it truly does become second nature for students eventually. Keep facilitating the process until you see evidence that they are ready to begin taking on some of the process on their own. Depending on the grade level you teach, your students may or may not ever reach this level. Here is the recommended sequence by grade level:

- *Kindergarten.* At this level, teachers are introducing the strategies one at a time, which takes a considerable amount of time. For this reason, reciprocal teaching is a teacher-led whole-class exercise through the course of the year.

- *First grade.* The sequence for first grade follows much of the same sequence as kindergarten. However, by the middle to end of the year, depending on the class, students may be reading independently and ready to start taking on some of the facilitation of reciprocal teaching. Nevertheless, this sequence will still take place in a whole-class setting.

- *Second and third grades.* Follow the same sequence, but with student facilitation beginning after about a month of teacher-directed work in third grade and after about two months in second grade.

- *Grades 4 and above.* Follow the same sequence, but pay close attention to student cues that will let you know when students are ready to take on more of the facilitation themselves.

Once students have reached an acceptable level of proficiency with the four strategies, you can begin to relinquish the process to them using the following process:

1. Students will work in cooperative groups of no more than four per group. Ensure that the groups are well balanced in terms of language learners, native English speakers, and different reading abilities. Do not isolate language learners into one group. They have a greater opportunity of success when they have English-speaking role models to help them negotiate the language.

2. Each person in the group is assigned one of the strategies, and they should have the appropriate strategy card in front of them. Before beginning the official reciprocal

How to Reach and Teach English Language Learners

teaching process, give students an opportunity to preread the text by reading all the titles, headings, and subheadings. Everyone is now ready to begin.

3. Although you no longer need to lead the process, the students still need someone to walk them from one step to the other. Therefore, each group of four selects a group leader who will lead the process. Your role now is to move the students from one strategy to the next so that the class is completing the process simultaneously. This need not remain permanently in place but only long enough to ensure that all groups are equally adept at carrying out the steps. Use the reciprocal teaching bookmarks in Form 20.2 or, for English learners at lower levels of language acquisition, create bookmarks with symbols for each step and sentence starters.

Prepare to see some amazing leadership skills evolve from this process. More exciting yet, you will see your students actively engaged in reading even textbooks. They have learned that it is preferable to read with a purpose than without one.

Form 20.2 Reciprocal Teaching Bookmarks

Reciprocal Teaching Steps	Reciprocal Teaching Steps	Reciprocal Teaching Steps	Reciprocal Teaching Steps
1. Predict What do I think will happen next? What do the clues show me might happen?	**1. Predict** What do I think will happen next? What do the clues show me might happen?	**1. Predict** What do I think will happen next? What do the clues show me might happen?	**1. Predict** What do I think will happen next? What do the clues show me might happen?
2. Question Is there a question I think will be answered in this section? I wonder if I will learn about _____?	**2. Question** Is there a question I think will be answered in this section? I wonder if I will learn about _____?	**2. Question** Is there a question I think will be answered in this section? I wonder if I will learn about _____?	**2. Question** Is there a question I think will be answered in this section? I wonder if I will learn about _____?
3. Read Remember to check your predictions and see if they are correct. If they aren't, make new predictions. Read to find answers to your questions.	**3. Read** Remember to check your predictions and see if they are correct. If they aren't, make new predictions. Read to find answers to your questions.	**3. Read** Remember to check your predictions and see if they are correct. If they aren't, make new predictions. Read to find answers to your questions.	**3. Read** Remember to check your predictions and see if they are correct. If they aren't, make new predictions. Read to find answers to your questions.
4. Clarify I still don't understand what this means. This word or section is unclear to me.	**4. Clarify** I still don't understand what this means. This word or section is unclear to me.	**4. Clarify** I still don't understand what this means. This word or section is unclear to me.	**4. Clarify** I still don't understand what this means. This word or section is unclear to me.
5. Summarize What is this main idea? What was this section about?	**5. Summarize** What is this main idea? What was this section about?	**5. Summarize** What is this main idea? What was this section about?	**5. Summarize** What is this main idea? What was this section about?

Taken from *How to Reach and Teach English Language Learners* by Rachel Carrillo Syrja, copyright © 2011 by John Wiley & Sons, Inc.

How to Reach and Teach English Language Learners

The Strategy: Creating Mental Images Through Visualization

It is important to teach students that authors use descriptive language to help us visualize what's happening in the story. These mental images also help us to comprehend what we are reading.

The Strategy in Action: Domains L and S

1. Begin with a short text selection that contains lots of descriptive language. Poetry is a good genre for teaching visualization. As you read, ask students to pay attention to the descriptive words and phrases. Be sure to cover any illustrations in the text so that students have to depend on the language to help them "see" what's happening in the story.

2. After reading the selection, have students work with a partner to identify descriptive words they hear. Remind them that descriptive language helps us visualize what is happening in a story, where it takes place, and what the characters look like. Then ask the partners to share descriptive words they heard. Chart their responses on large chart paper. Using the think-aloud strategy, add any words they may have missed.

3. Have students draw what they were able to visualize as a result of the descriptive language used in the selection. Have them share their drawings; then uncover the illustrations from the text so that they can see how close they got. Have students share their drawings with a partner and compare any similarities or differences in their visualizations. This is an opportunity for students to see how our schema and prior knowledge influence the way each of us "sees" the text.

The Strategy: Interactive Reading

Once students have had sufficient direct instruction in reciprocal teaching and have internalized the strategies of predicting, questioning, clarifying, and summarizing, they can move on to interactive reading, which reinforces reading with a purpose.

The Strategy in Action: Domains L, S, R, W, and T

1. Explain to students that there are three stages to reading—before, during, and after—and that good readers are actively engaged during all three stages. They are now going to read with a partner up to a specified point in the text.

2. Before reading, the students individually record on their handout (Form 20.3) predictions and questions regarding the text. They next share their predictions and questions with their partner and then read up to a predetermined part of the text. They are encouraged to search for answers to their questions as they read and record those in the second column of their handout.

3. Once they reach the end of the section they have been assigned to read, students work together to revise their predictions, confirm the answers to their questions, and determine any new questions. Students are then assigned a final portion of the text to read.

4. At the conclusion of reading, students again revisit their predictions, record any new or unanswered questions on the handout, and work together to write a summary of what was read.

How to Reach and Teach English Language Learners

Form 20.3 Interactive Reading Handout

Before I Read	While I Read	After I Read
Predictions	Modified Predictions	New Questions
Questions	Answers to Questions	Summary
	New Questions	

Word Recognition

Reading fluency and a wide vocabulary make up one of the six main building blocks of reading: word recognition. In fact, if a student lacks either of these essential skills, then other comprehension techniques and strategies, such as summarizing, predicting and confirming, questioning, and clarifying lose their effectiveness and yield meager results.

Fluency

In order to comprehend text, students must have the ability to read fluently and accurately. By the end of third grade, students should be able to decode every word in their *meaning vocabulary*, that is, the words that he or she has been exposed to through oral language experiences. In kindergarten, students gain their meaning vocabulary through listening to and retelling stories. Once they become fluent readers, they gain their meaning vocabulary through direct instruction or independent reading.

Research has shown that students who cannot read text at 100 words per minute with 95 percent accuracy by the end of third grade will have difficulty reading.

In order to find out whether your English learners are reading fluently, you may need to assess them. Most schools conduct reading fluency assessments a few times per year, but it's possible you may not have access to the results. In that case, here is a basic accuracy and fluency test that you can conduct yourself with just these materials:

- Grade-level passage or book
- Teacher and student copies
- Pencil
- Stopwatch or watch with a second hand
- Calculator

Provide the student with a copy of the grade-level passage. Be sure to have a clean copy of the text for each student since they will use this copy to record errors and total number of words read. In order to facilitate the computation of fluency, your copy should have the number of words in each line of text indicated at the end of each line in the text.

Set the timer for one minute and have the student read the text aloud to you. As he or she reads, cross out any words that the student reads incorrectly, as well as the point at which the child stops reading at the end of one minute.

In order to compute the student's accuracy, subtract the number of errors (E) from the number of running words (RW) and then divide by the number of running words: $RW - E/RW$. For this assessment, errors are mispronunciations, substitutions, reversals, omissions, or words you supply if the student makes no attempt to read the word.

To compute the fluency rate, that is, the correct number of words per minute (CWPM), subtract the number of errors (E) from the number of running words read in one minute (RW1): $RW1 - E = CWPM$.

Each state's standards contain fluency benchmarks for proficiency particularly at the elementary levels. The fluency scores listed here are generic and meant only as a starting point:

	Elementary End-of-Year Fluency Benchmarks	Approaching Benchmark Fluency Scores
Grade 1	60 WPM	55 WPM
Grade 2	95 WPM	80 WPM
Grade 3	114 WPM	94 WPM
Grade 4	118 WPM	110 WPM
Grade 5	128 WPM	120 WPM

Vocabulary Development

Research shows that children raised in low-income households begin school with much more limited vocabularies than their high-income peers do. Three-year-olds from middle- and high-income families have a vocabulary of up to twelve hundred words in contrast to their low-income peers who may know as few as six hundred words.[19] Research shows that by second grade, children from low-income families are as much as 60 percent behind the average student in reading ability.[20] Lack of vocabulary development is a major contributor to this literacy gap. While learning vocabulary in rich and meaningful contexts is essential, research also suggests that children need fifteen to twenty exposures to a word to make it their own.

Students need to learn three thousand to four thousand new words every year. Estimates have shown that students who read just twenty minutes a day can learn between one thousand and four thousand new words per year.[21] Enriching your school's independent reading program by investing in books from several languages and language levels could help provide extended opportunities for wide reading in school. Another possibility is to develop a book-in-a-bag program in which students can check out "books in a bag" to read at home. Anything we can do to increase the amount of wide reading students do will have a large, positive impact on their fluency and vocabulary development.

Several researchers have found a scarcity of systematic, intentional vocabulary and language teaching, a dismaying trend that has also been documented in programs serving English learners.[22] Dutro and Moran, and Fillmore and Snow, emphasize that simply exposing second language students to interactive, English-language-rich classrooms is insufficient.[23] In fact, in order for language-minority students to attain rigorous content standards, intensive instruction of academic vocabulary and related grammatical knowledge must be carefully orchestrated across the subject areas for these students to attain rigorous content standards.[24]

This situation can be remedied in the following ways:

- *Encourage wide reading.* Vocabulary grows as a consequence of independent reading and increasing reading volume.[25]

- *Direct-teach important individual words.* Students learn new words using various teacher-directed instructional strategies.[26]

- *Teach word learning strategies.* Students independently learn new words when they use strategies such as exploring context and analyzing prefixes.[27]

- *Foster word consciousness.* Vocabulary develops when students engage in various activities to increase language play, word choice in writing, and sensitivity to word parts.[28]

The Strategy: Repeated Reading

English learners from all language proficiency levels can benefit greatly from repeated reading. For those at beginning levels who may not feel at ease reading out loud, provide them with text they can take home and practice without the anxiety of being in the classroom. Keep in mind that many of these students have limited access to books at home.

The Strategy in Action: Domains L, S, and R

1. Repeated reading for authentic purposes. Have students:

    - Practice reading a favorite part of a book.

    - Practice reading a picture book that you will read later to a younger child.

    - Practice reading a favorite part of a book aloud to classmates.

    - Memorize a favorite poem or part of the book.

2. Timed readings

    - Time each student for two minutes as he or she reads a short text repeatedly. Students keep an individual tally showing their progress in fluency over the course of the week. Work on the same piece of text several times over the week. Students keep track of and graph their improvement in fluency over time.

    - Time students individually on a passage they can read that is at their instructional or independent level. Students color in a graph showing the number of words they read in one minute on this text. Help the students set a words-per-minute goal that they can work toward over a period of time.

Students practice until they meet their goal. Then time them reading the text for one minute. They color in the graph to reflect their gains in fluency on this text. The student then works on a new text selection that is at the same level or slightly more challenging.

3. Wide reading during independent reading time. Each child selects books during independent reading time that are at his or her independent reading level (95 to 100 percent accuracy). In order for students to develop maximum fluency, they should be reading at their independent level.

The Strategy: Key Vocabulary Prediction

Key vocabulary prediction provides language learners with an opportunity to list the words they know prior to learning and then slowly watch the list grow as they acquire more content and academic vocabulary. Form 20.4 provides alphabet boxes for the vocabulary.

Form 20.4 Alphabet Boxes for Vocabulary

A–B	C–D	E–F	G–H

I–J	K–L	M–N	O–P

Q–R	S–T	U–V	WXYZ

The Strategy in Action: Domains L, S, R, W, and T

1. Introduce the subject or topic of instruction, and give your students sticky notes. As a way of connecting with students' prior knowledge, ask them to think of any words that they may know that they might find in the following pages in the book. Give them some think time to try to pull as much vocabulary as they can from their memory. They then write the words they've thought of on the stickies.

2. After about five minutes, pair students up and have them compare their lists and discuss some of the meanings of the listed words.

3. Have students return to their seats, and make sure they've listed all the words they and their partner came up with initially on their own copy of Form 20.4.

4. Project a blank copy of Form 20.4 and ask students to share the vocabulary they've listed, beginning with the letter A. Encourage every student to contribute a vocabulary word. When students share, they must say the word and how they know it is associated with the topic. Then add each word to the projected whole-class alphabet chart. Levels 1 and 2 English learners, who may be hesitant to speak in front of the class, can bring you their sticky with a word written on it or a sketch of a concept or word associated with this topic so that you can record it on the class chart.

5. When all of the words have been shared and put on the class chart, project it on the SMART board or overhead projector so that all students can see it. Ask students to work with a shoulder partner to predict what they think the reading will be about based on the vocabulary they brainstormed.

6. You can decide at this point whether to have students develop questions about the topic now or prior to reading the next day.

7. The next day, after having completed the formulation of questions and the reading of the text, students can revisit the alphabet chart. They volunteer new vocabulary they encountered in the reading and add it to the chart.

8. Students add new vocabulary to their vocabulary notebooks.

The Strategy: Word Maps

Word maps are a strategy that uses a graphic organizer as a way of teaching and learning new vocabulary students encounter during content-area instruction. English learners particularly benefit from this strategy because of the rich vocabulary development that takes place as they complete the organizer.

The Strategy in Action: Domains L, S, R, W, and T

1. Give students multiple copies of the word map graphic organizer in Form 20.5.

Form 20.5 Sample Word Map Template

What this word is . . .   What this word isn't . . .

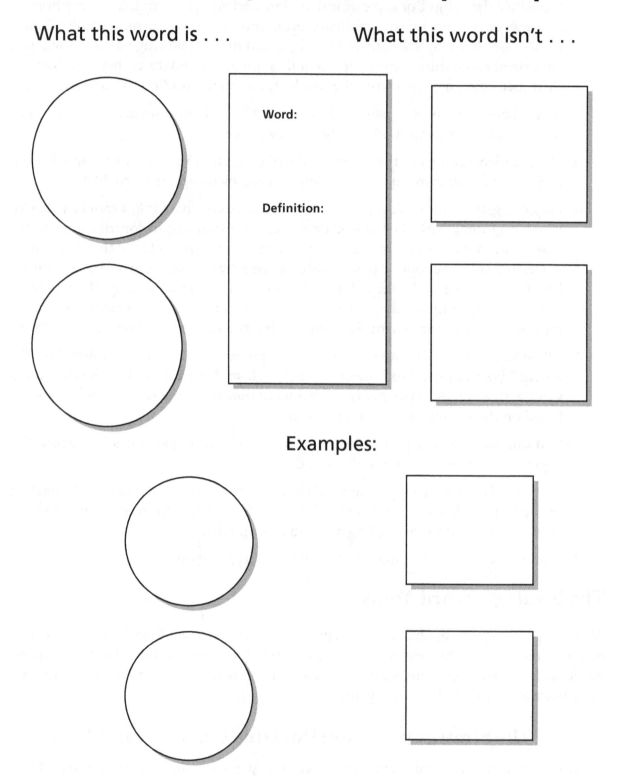

Word:

Definition:

Examples:

Source: Adapted from Beers (2003).

How to Reach and Teach English Language Learners

2. Before introducing the text to the class, identify three to five vocabulary words critical to understanding the story. Then give each student a copy of Form 20.5 for each word. Once students have sufficient experience with this strategy, they will no longer need to use the reproducible and can complete the activity using a blank sheet of paper. Students write the word, its part of speech, and a definition in the center box. Beginning-level English learners can draw a picture.

3. Next, students write a synonym for the word (or draw an example of what the word is) in the circles and antonyms of the word, or what the word isn't in the squares. They then write or draw examples in the circles and nonexamples in the squares.

4. Students share what they wrote or illustrated with a partner.

Wide Reading: The Importance of Independent Reading

As I researched this topic, it became clear that wide reading has an exponential effect on increased achievement. A question that persisted was how English learners can keep up with their native English-speaking classmates when most of them live in poverty and have limited access to books. It didn't take long to realize that the majority of opportunities to read widely would have to take place in class. One program that aims to increase the amount of time students read in school is independent reading. Independent reading is a form of wide reading in which students select high-interest books that are at their independent and instructional reading levels. While we know the positive effects that independent reading has on achievement in all content areas, we also know that children who read the most tend to score the highest on informal and formal assessment measures.[29]

Independent reading has five key characteristics:[30]

1. The teacher provides guidance in the students' text selections.

2. Students keep track of what they read.

3. Students reflect on what they read.

4. Teacher and students participate in mini-lessons tied to reading comprehension and book discussions from time to time.

5. The teacher is not reading during the entire reading block unless he or she is modeling a strategy with a student.

Studies supporting independent reading have found that students tend to be more engaged during reading time when they reflect on what they have read. Studies have also shown that engaging in discourse and discussion during reading time can be beneficial for students' reading achievement, as well as attitudes about reading.

The Strategy: Implementing Independent Reading

When you implement independent reading at any grade level, make sure that the following guidelines are in place:

- Make independent reading a daily part of your curriculum.

- Assess literacy levels in students' primary language in order to determine their independent, instruction, and frustration reading levels:

  - *Independent reading level:* Reading feels effortless. The student can read and understand without assistance, accurately decoding 99 percent of words and comprehending with 95 to 100 percent accuracy.

  - *Instruction reading level:* The material is somewhat difficult and requires more active reading and some assistance. The student can accurately decode 95 percent of the words and comprehend with 90 to 94 percent accuracy.

  - *Frustration reading level:* The material is too difficult for the student to read accurately even with teacher assistance. The student can accurately decode below 90 percent and comprehend with less than 89 percent accuracy.

- Assess students' literacy levels in English, and determine their independent, instruction, and frustration reading levels.

- Help English learners select books that are at the appropriate reading level for them.

- Provide frequent opportunities for students to be able to reflect on what they've read orally or in writing.

- Motivate students to read independently by reading aloud to them on a regular basis, even at the high school level. Choose these books based on your students' interests. (See the interest surveys in the Part Five Resources section.)

The Strategy in Action: Domains L, S, R, W, and T

1. Organize your classroom library by reading levels and genres in English and other languages.

2. Encourage English learners to read books in their primary language. Ensure that you have a good selection of books that are high interest, culturally relevant, and for different readability levels. Inquire about grants or community donations to help build your classroom library, particularly if you lack books in languages other than English.

3. In order to keep your bookshelves from becoming disorganized, create book boxes from which students can choose reading material. Rotate titles in and out as you notice students running out of books to read.

4. Add any student published writing, in English and other languages, to your library or book boxes. In the upper grades, you may want to remove students' identifying information. Students love reading each other's writing. This will have a positive impact on their reading and spill over into writing as they begin to look forward to writing something that can be added to the classroom library.

5. Do not force students to finish a book. Although you certainly want to discourage students from continuously changing books, keep in mind that this is supposed to be recreational reading and should not become a chore for students. Use this as a way to show students that even adults start books and change books. It's part of being a reader!

6. Have students keep track every day of the books they read and reflect about what they read. Form 20.6 provides a log for elementary school students (K–5) and Form 20.7 for secondary students (grades 6–12). Level 1 students, who have limited English language skills, can use Form 20.8 to draw pictures to reflect what they read about during independent reading time. Level 2 students may use Form 20.9 to draw pictures reflecting what they read about and write one- or two-word descriptions of each picture.

7. Encourage students to share their independent reading reflections with a partner of their choosing every day.

8. Occasionally conduct mini-lessons on comprehension strategies and use independent reading time to model the strategy by using think-alouds.

Form 20.6 Independent Reading Log for Grades K–5

Name _____

Date	Title	Start page	End page	Total pages read

How to Reach and Teach English Language Learners

Form 20.7 Independent Reading Log for Grades 6–12

Name _____

Date	Title and Brief Description	Language	Reading Level: (I)Independent (IS)Instruction (F)Frustration	Total pages read

Form 20.8 Independent Reading Reflection, Level 1

Name _____

How to Reach and Teach English Language Learners

Form 20.9 Independent Reading Reflection, Level 2

Name _____

Chapter 21

Strategies for Writing

In This Chapter

- Review of the research on writing and English learners
- The importance of connecting reading and writing
- Writing strategies

Learning to write is a significant part of becoming literate in any language. Because of the high levels of cognition demanded by writing, it is often one of the last domains to fully develop. Research has focused heavily on how children and adults learn to write.[1] What this research has revealed is that children learn to write by writing.[2] In other words, the more writing a child does, the better he or she becomes at it. This seems to suggest, just as recent research has, that writing every day in every content area matters.[3] This is particularly significant for English learners who may be developing their skills in writing. Rather than hold off on writing until they have achieved a higher level of language acquisition, we should be providing opportunities for writing daily.

Writing for most young children consists of drawing and scribbling. With time, their writing matures and takes on a more sophisticated form. The development of these early writing skills can be fostered through the use of a flexible process that involves selecting a topic, drafting, revising, editing, and publishing.[4] This is often referred to as the *writing process,* although not all educators agree on terminology.

It appears that English learners pass through similar developmental stages in writing. In the early stages of language acquisition, their writing may not seem very sophisticated; however, with time and practice, the writing improves until it begins to approximate that of a native English speaker. The most effective way to teach this process is for the teacher to model it through shared writing.[5]

A Word About Grammar and Usage

An extensive body of research addresses the effects of the teaching of grammar and usage as a vehicle for improved writing. Hillocks and Smith have found that the study of grammar has no impact on writing quality.[6] What children and young adults need to know about grammar and usage is simply that they learn best through writing, not through the tedious and boring study of grammar.[7] If students have difficulty with a particular element of grammar or usage in their writing, the most effective way to help the child is to give him or her a brief mini-lesson focusing on this specific element, using the student's own writing or a piece of literature to model the correct use.[8]

Since thinking is a critical part of meaning construction, classrooms that foster meaning construction through reading and writing will produce better thinkers.[9] Therefore, as is the case with reading, writing is and should be an integral part of all content areas. In science, social studies, reading and English language arts, and mathematics, students demonstrate their response to knowledge taught, concept attainment, and understanding through writing.

Writing in the Content Areas

Writing across the content areas has been shown to be one of the highest-yielding strategies that can be implemented in any classroom.[10] The implication of the research is that students should be writing every day and in every content area. Even at a time when so many teachers are feeling overburdened by the demands and expectations on instructional time, we cannot afford to ignore the implementation of nonfiction writing.

The Strategy: Implementing Writing Across the Curriculum

Implementation of nonfiction writing across the curriculum presents many challenges, and one is the resistance of some content-area teachers to allot any of their classroom instructional time in order to make room for ten to fifteen minutes of writing. The first task is to reassure all educators that time spent on writing can be considered anything but a loss of time. The ability to write about a topic requires deep knowledge and understanding of that topic. Therefore, providing time each day for students to write in the content areas will result in improved levels of learning for all.

When planning a writing assignment, consider the writing levels of your English learners because it would be inappropriate to expect them all to be able to write in the same fashion as your native English speakers. Let's say you have a level 3 speech emergence student and a level 4 intermediate fluency student in your social studies class. The WIDA Can Do statements for those two levels read as follows:

Writing Level 3
Engage in prewriting strategies (for example, the use of graphic organizers).
Form simple sentences using word and phrase banks.
Participate in interactive journal writing.
Give content-based information using visuals or graphics.

Writing Level 4
Produce original sentences.
Create messages for social purposes, such as get-well cards.
Compose journal entries about personal experiences.
Use classroom resources such as picture dictionaries to compose sentences.

The Strategy in Action: Domains S, R, W, and T

1. Plan writing experiences that are reflective of what your English learners can do according to their language acquisition levels. For example, implement a daily journal in content-area classes at all grade levels, and provide time each day for students to write about their learning, ask questions, or comment on something they heard during the lesson. Set appropriate objectives aligned to the students' current levels of language acquisition.

2. If students are using a daily journal, level 3 English learners will be expected, according to the WIDA standards, to form simple sentences using word/phrase banks and to participate in interactive journal writing. This lets the teacher know that although the level 3 student will be able to work on the interactive journal with the rest of the class, the standard requires that the teacher provide him or her with a word and phrase bank as a way of scaffolding the writing assignment.

3. The level 4 English learner will be expected, according to the WIDA standards, to "compose journal entries about personal experiences and use classroom resources (for example, picture dictionaries) to compose sentences." Again, although level 4

English learners will be able to participate in the journal-entry writing assignment, they will require support in the form of classroom resources, such as picture dictionaries, to help them compose sentences.

4. Offer students the opportunity to share their reflections or writings with their classmates.

The English language proficiency writing standards also provide some invaluable information about the resources English learners require, including in this case the word bank and picture dictionaries. Your state's writing standards can help to inform the specific writing assignments for these learners; more important, they also help shape expectations for what students at these levels can produce in writing.

The Strategy: Connecting Reading and Writing Through Content

In this strategy, the teacher uses content and the reading done with content to help build vocabulary for English learners and help them use that vocabulary to write about what they've learned. In the following Strategy in Action, the teacher is using writing as the vehicle for teaching synonyms and antonyms.

The Strategy in Action: Domains L, S, R, W, and T

1. Prior to the writing assignment, decide what type of vocabulary you would like your students to practice using and teach that vocabulary during ESL or language arts. For example, if you are teaching synonyms, ask students to brainstorm synonyms for *happy* and for *angry*. List the synonyms for *happy* on a piece of yellow construction paper and the synonyms for *angry* on a piece of red construction paper (Figure 21.1).

2. After completing the brainstorm, combine the charts and tape them back to back so that the yellow side shows the synonyms of *happy* and the red side antonyms of *happy*. It is much easier for English learners to come up with synonyms than antonyms, which is why I advise brainstorming synonyms. If you had asked for antonyms of *happy*, your students may have struggled to come up with words. In this way, you can physically show students how the synonyms listed for *angry* are the opposite of the words listed for *happy*, which is the meaning of antonyms.

3. Have students work with a partner to write sentences using words from each poster. The students read their sentences to each other and then share them with the whole class if they feel comfortable doing so.

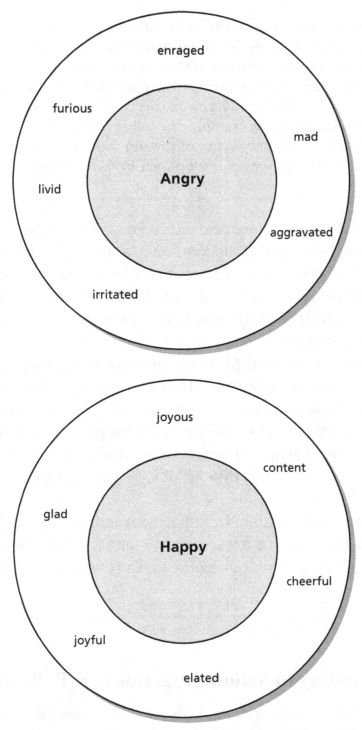

Figure 21.1 Sample Brainstorm

The Strategy: Developing Voice

Developing voice in writing is one of the most difficult parts of writing. *Voice* is defined as the quality that makes an author's writing unique and conveys his or her personality and character. Teachers can use the content they are reading and learning about and have students write from the perspective of one of the topics they are studying. For example, if students are studying the civil rights movement, they could write facts from the perspective of Dr. Martin Luther King Jr. In the example that follows, third graders are learning about the sun and will write from the perspective of the sun. Not only is this strategy engaging, but it also helps students learn how to develop voice in their writing.

> Ms. Wieler's third graders are learning facts about the sun in their science book. She has provided each pair of students with a low-readability text, and the students are working with their partners to list facts they learn about the sun. After they have finished, the pairs share their facts with the rest of the class. Ms. Wieler records the facts on chart paper or document camera so that all students can see the facts collected.
>
> Next, she asks the students to choose an emotion from a previously brainstormed list of vocabulary and write about their sun facts from that emotion. In this example, students choose emotions from their happy or angry chart and then use those words to write sentences from the perspective of the sun—for example, "I am very happy that my rays help plants grow on Earth." In this way, students continue through their list of facts and write those facts from the perspective of the sun.
>
> The students now have lists of facts that they can illustrate and share with the class. They read their sun facts to each other. Then Ms. Wieler compiles the facts into a class book, and students can choose to read the book during independent reading time.

The Strategy in Action: Domains L, S, R, W, and T

1. After explaining to students the topic they will be learning about, collect relevant books and other resources from which students gather facts. The students work as partners, reading their text and collecting facts.

2. Each pair of students then shares their facts with the whole class, and you record them on chart paper or a document camera.

3. Refer to the brainstormed list of emotion vocabulary from the previous day, and have students write facts from the perspective of the topic they are learning about. In the scenario, students have the sun take on the emotions from the vocabulary list, and they write from the perspective of the sun. This exercise teaches them about voice and also gives the class an opportunity to work with common vocabulary.

4. Compile the students' writing in a class book, and add it to the classroom library.

5. In a variation of this strategy, students brainstorm different emotions and the vocabulary that goes with them. You can also give them sentence frames depending on their English language level. An example of a brainstormed list of emotions and sentence frames could include the following:

> *Joy:* "I am so pleased that ..."; "I am happy to be able to ..."
>
> *Fear:* "I'm afraid that ..."; "I'm scared that ..."
>
> *Surprise:* "Can you believe that ..."; "I am so shocked that ..."
>
> *Anger:* "I am so angry that ..."; "Unfortunately ..."
>
> *Sadness:* "I'm sad to say ..."; "It saddens me that ..."
>
> *Love:* "I love that ..."; "I adore that ..."

This connection between reading and writing helps students use the information and vocabulary they are reading about in their content areas in a genuine context that is also fun for them.

The Strategy: RAFT (Role, Audience, Format, Topic) Writing

RAFT is an acronym used to describe the four critical ingredients of writing:

R   Role of the writer
A   Audience for the writing
F   Format the writing will take
T   Topic covered in the writing

The RAFT strategy provides support in strategic reading and writing. It helps students think critically and creatively about the content they are studying; make connections to events, people, times, and places they are reading about; and be able to synthesize all of that information into a creative piece of writing.

Allen states that RAFT writing can be used in any content area that students have studied or read about a topic, concept, or event.[11] For English learners, it would be important to brainstorm vocabulary and add to that vocabulary through a strategy such as list-group-label in Chapter Twenty so that they feel supported when writing.

The Strategy in Action: Domains R, W, and T

1. After learning about a particular topic or event, you use the RAFT organizer (Form 21.1) to have students brainstorm all the possible roles they could take on as writers. For example, students who are learning about the Middle Ages use their knowledge of the topic to brainstorm the possible roles.

2. You and the students then complete the graphic, brainstorming the audience for their writing, the format their writing will take, and the topical information they will include in their writing.

3. From the brainstormed list, students complete their own RAFT organizer. Students are now ready to begin writing.

When planning the use of RAFT, don't forget to take into account the writing language acquisition levels of your students, and plan appropriate scaffolds and supports for them. For example, levels 1 and 2 students would be completing the writing assignment using a CLOZE (sentence frames with strategically placed fill-in-the-blanks) and illustrations. Level 3 students require additional support, such as an extensive word bank, and those at level 4 and above should be able to complete the assignment as illustrated here. Plan in advance for these modifications.

The writing produced through the use of RAFT can be used as a culminating writing assignment, for assessment purposes, or as a lead-in into a related unit of study.

Form 21.1 RAFT Organizer

Taken from *How to Reach and Teach English Language Learners* by Rachel Carrillo Syrja, copyright © 2011 by John Wiley & Sons, Inc.

Name _____

R	A
F	**T**

R   Role. What role will you assume in this piece of writing?

A   Audience. Who will be your audience? What is the time period?

F   Format. What format will you use: article, poem, letter, comic strip, or short story?

T   Topic. What details from the topic of study will you include in your writing? What questions will be answered or what points will you make?

Chapter 22

Strategies for Math

In This Chapter

- A review of the research on teaching math to English learners
- Common difficulties English learners have in math
- Preinstruction strategies
- During-instruction strategies
- Postinstruction strategies

Despite what conventional wisdom has suggested, teaching mathematics to English learners is fraught with complexity. For far too long, many educators have taught from the mistaken assumption that English learners have less of a struggle in math because, they say, "Math is primarily numbers." That theory does not hold true. Those who teach math, particularly at the middle and high school levels, know that math is rich in language and vocabulary, and English learners often struggle because of their lack of academic vocabulary. In fact, the achievement gap widens substantially in the areas of knowledge and skills, mathematics understanding, and application as students get older.[1]

Interestingly, the gap is not significant until the middle elementary grades, and then it continues to increase in the subsequent grade levels.[2]

In his study on the effect of language on the teaching of mathematics, Khisty theorized that the widening gap could be attributed to the fact that mathematics becomes more word laden, thus requiring students to be able to interpret and translate words into mathematical symbols and operations. Mathematics understanding and application, which takes the form of problem solving in the classroom, clearly requires a stronger conceptual foundation than does straightforward computation. Language plays an important role in a student's ability to understand and apply mathematics—first, in the comprehension of questions, and second, in the elementary years when children are developing conceptual understanding. The middle grades appear to be a turning point because it is here where the traditional emphasis in mathematics learning shifts from simple whole number facts to more conceptually complex numbers, concepts, and skills.[3]

A major contributing factor to English learners' struggle in mathematics has to do with our tendency to teach math as a series of steps or procedures. We define the procedural approach to teaching mathematics as a set of steps to take to solve a problem. This approach quickly introduces students to traditionally accepted algorithms or steps. Although doing mathematics requires some knowledge of algorithms, it also requires a good deal of conceptual understanding in order to know why and how to undertake the steps. In other words, it is not enough to know procedures. Unfortunately, when teachers see students, particularly English learners, quickly mimic the procedure modeled, they assume proficiency; in fact, the student has learned only the process, not the concept. This lack of conceptual understanding shows up in the form of persistent misconceptions and errors as students move toward the application of mathematics in the middle and high school years. Although educators have long recommended that we teach math conceptually, the procedural emphasis prevails in many classrooms. This approach presents challenges for all students, especially English learners. Their lack of academic vocabulary contributes to and compounds their lack of conceptual understanding, making achievement in mathematics difficult, and perhaps unattainable.

How to Help English Learners Achieve in Math

Every teacher, beginning in kindergarten, plays a vital role in the development of a student's mathematical understanding. It is essential, then, that we approach the teaching of mathematics as a language in itself. O'Malley and Chamot write:

> For the child who has to begin to learn in a second language, whether on entering school or later, the linguistic concepts and structures have to be taught.... Unless the linguistic concepts are presented in concrete and dynamic form, the language used by the teacher will only be a mystery to the hearer. This means that mathematics must not be taught by the teacher writing symbols on the blackboard, rearranging them, getting

"answers", asking the class to copy the process and to learn it by heart. Instead the teacher must be trained to involve the children in carefully structured activities, investigations and discussions which will ensure understanding. In short, the teaching of mathematics in a second language must, in effect, adopt the principles which govern the methods of teaching a second language as a language.[4]

Chamot recommends that the curriculum and its objectives be used as the framework for instruction in the second language.[5] We should conduct a special analysis of the language functions and the math-specific understandings required for success in mathematics at every grade level. The vocabulary and language skills necessary to achieve the objectives should then be identified and incorporated into our teaching.

O'Malley and Chamot also suggests that students who have been identified as English learners should be assessed in the different content areas to determine their proficiency in the language functions required in each one.[6] The mathematics curriculum should then be revised to include attention to the development of the language skills that students with limited proficiency in English require. The mathematics teacher then becomes not necessarily an ESL teacher but rather a teacher of the language needed for students to learn mathematical concepts and skills. This deliberate approach to teaching the language skills and vocabulary necessary for success will help to ensure that students are able to access the content and then learn the concepts underlying the processes in mathematics.

Difficulties That English Learners Face in Math

In addition to lacking the language structures and vocabulary of mathematics in English, students who have come to the United States from other countries may have learned different processes in their native countries from those we follow in mathematics here.[7] These are some of the common differences that can lead to misconceptions:

- The formation of numbers may vary.

- A different use of the decimal from ours. In some countries, large numbers are written with decimals rather than commas, as in 134.765 versus 134,765.

- The measurement system common to the United States, which differs from the rest of the world, may be a particular challenge for older English learners.

- Most English learners have learned math by rote memorization.

- Many students may be accustomed to mental calculations, which means that they may not have been required to show work when calculating, or they may show work in a different way.

- Fractions may be unfamiliar to ELLs, especially if decimals received more emphasis than fractions in their native country.

- In some cases, they have learned algorithms differently from the way they are learned in the United States. This may be especially true for some English learner students who were older when they arrived in the United States. Rather than forbid them to use a different algorithm, allow students the opportunity to share. Students can learn a lot from each other by comparing algorithms and analyzing similarities and differences. Although the standard algorithm represents an efficient way to solve a math problem, there are several strategies that students may use to solve a problem.

- Geometry in particular has many terms that may cause difficulties in understanding. For example, the word *right* in "right angle" has a completely different meaning from the meanings regarding direction and correctness with which ELLs may already be familiar.[8]

Strategies for Math

What becomes clear from the research is that English learners require intensive support in mathematics vocabulary as well as understanding math conceptually rather than as a series of steps to follow by rote. The strategies we examine here divide the instructional sequence into three distinct parts: preinstruction, during instruction, and postinstruction.

Preinstruction Strategies

Lessons should begin by considering the vocabulary and prerequisite knowledge that English learners need to have in place prior to the lesson.[9]

The Strategy: Previewing the Lesson

Students should be taught to preview the text, vocabulary, and text features as a way of connecting to the content and preparing to learn the new information. This strategy, used quite often in other content areas, needs to be used more in math.

The Strategy in Action: Domains L, S, R, W, and T

1. Either list the sections of the book on the board that students will preview in the lesson or have students use an advance organizer. They can preview the following:

   - Section title

   - Vocabulary

- Examples
- Guiding questions or big ideas

2. Previewing can be done by the whole class, especially in the early elementary grades, or by groups or pairs.

3. After completing their preview of the lesson, students write questions they may have prior to learning the content. Again, as in reading, these questions help to set a purpose for the learning that is about to take place. Students can work with partners and then share their questions with their partner prior to sharing it with the class if they so choose. A good strategy is to have students construct a chart with questions on one side and notes on the other (see Form 22.1). As the learning is taking place, you or the students can complete the chart.

Form 22.1 Organizer for Questions and Notes

Questions	Notes

Taken from *How to Reach and Teach English Language Learners* by Rachel Carrillo Syrja, copyright © 2011 by John Wiley & Sons, Inc.

How to Reach and Teach English Language Learners

4. Students are taught to listen for answers to their questions within the lesson. When they hear those answers, they note them in the chart. It is important to provide clues and wait time to allow students the opportunity to record notes.

5. At the end of the lesson, students can volunteer to share the answers to the questions that they discovered in their learning.

The Strategy: Vocabulary Instruction for Multiple-Meaning Words

Language register is the term linguists use to refer to the meanings that serve a particular function in the language, as well as the words and structures that convey those meanings. In math, *mathematics register* refers to the meanings belonging to the natural language used in mathematics. Halliday suggested that a mathematics register is composed of natural language words that are reinterpreted in the context of mathematics, such as *right, point, field,* and *even*; terms created from combinations of natural language words, such as *feedback* and *output*; and terms formed from combining elements of Greek and Latin words, such as *parabola, denominator,* and *coefficient*.[10] Although the tendency has been to think of mathematics as a subject that does not require a strong command of language, we now know that mathematical reasoning and problem solving are language laden and rely on a firm understanding of basic math vocabulary.

Both the ESL teacher and the mainstream teacher can use this strategy for learning multiple meaning words. It can be differentiated and used in any grade level and should be part of math instruction for all English learners.

Students are given vocabulary from an upcoming lesson or unit and are strategically taught the vocabulary that may have multiple meanings. Teaching the multiple meanings will help students better understand the mathematics in the lesson.

The Strategy in Action: Domains S, W, and T

1. During the planning stages of your lesson, survey the content for any multiple meaning vocabulary words, such as *right* and *table,* and add them to your list of vocabulary to preteach.

2. Use the vocabulary worksheet or any other tools you currently use to teach vocabulary. Give each student a copy of Form 22.2, and have them rate their current understanding of each word before learning, using the following ratings:

    ☺   I know this word and can use it in a sentence.
    :/   I've seen or heard this word, but I'm not sure if I really understand it.
    ?   I don't know this word.

You can use symbols or images for younger students or a number rating system from 1 to 3. This can also be done as a whole group for early elementary grades. You can share the word and then ask students to put their thumb up if they know the word, thumb sideways if they think they might know it, and thumb down if they don't know the word. They can then turn to their partner and share what they know about the word. In this way, you will gain some valuable insight into your students' current understanding of these important multiple-meaning math vocabulary words.

Form 22.2 Predicting Multiple-Meaning Words in Math

Name_____

Rate your knowledge of each word using the following symbols:

☺   I know this word.

:/   I've seen or heard this word but I don't really understand it.

?   I don't know this word.

Word	Rating Before Learning	Rating After Learning
_____	_____	_____
_____	_____	_____
_____	_____	_____

The words above have double meanings. You may know one of those meanings already or you may know both. Write down what you think this word means in math.

_____

_____

_____

_____

_____

_____

Strategies for Math

3. After students rate their understanding of the word, have them predict the meaning of the word within the context of mathematics. Encouraging students to make predictions allows them to make connections to their prior knowledge and thereby connect to the content you are presenting.

4. Have students work with a partner to write the word and the definition in their own words. For example, for the word *table,* students could write: "A piece of furniture where things can be placed on or where people can sit at and eat."

5. Then use realia to show students what the word *table* means in math. Have students share how they define the word *table* in math, and record some of the student-generated definitions on the board or on chart paper. Students then record the mathematical definition of the word in a math journal. They also draw an image that will remind them of what the word means in math. *Challenge:* Ask students to think about the word and predict whether it has any other meanings.

6. Students return to their ratings and reassess their knowledge of the word after instruction. They also revisit their prediction to confirm whether it was correct.

7. Have students practice using the vocabulary in context. Share an example of how the word might be used and challenge other students to come up with a sentence to share. They can share with their partners first and then with the whole group. It is critical the English learners have opportunities to practice using the vocabulary.

If you are working with older students, you may opt to use Form 22.3. Students can list multiple-meaning math vocabulary, the definition they are familiar with, and then the mathematical definition. They can then draw an image that will help them remember the meaning of the word in mathematics. Alternatively, students can record their work in a math journal.

Form 22.3 Multiple-Meaning Words

Name_____

Word: _____

Definition 1: _____

Math definition: _____

Visual clue:

Word: _____

Definition 1: _____

Math definition: _____

Visual clue:

Word: _____

Definition 1: _____

Math definition: _____

Visual clue:

During-Instruction Strategies

Once students are familiar with the vocabulary in the lesson, consider how you can make the content accessible to students at all levels of language acquisition. The strategies set out in this section can be used as presented or modified to fit the needs of your students.

The Strategy: Group Solutions

Although this may not seem like a typical math strategy, it holds many benefits for English learners. In my travels around the country, I have witnessed far too many traditional classrooms with students sitting quietly while the teacher talks, then students sitting quietly practicing the steps that their teacher just taught them. The level of disengagement and boredom in these classrooms is disheartening. I have also visited math classrooms that are alive with learning, with students interacting with the content and supported by cooperative structures that the teacher has put in place to ensure their success. For those who may not be comfortable with large groups, you can begin by having students work in groups to solve problems. The process that follows has been adapted from the work of Ainsworth and Christinson.[11]

The Strategy in Action: Domains L, S, R, W, and T

1. Strategically group or pair students. Have students who share a common language work together, and try to have students with a higher language acquisition level grouped or paired with students who have a lower language acquisition level. This will ensure that the student with limited English skills receives primary language support from another student. Try to acquire materials in as many primary languages as possible. Most publishers have materials in several languages. If you cannot get a copy of the textbook in the languages you need, you may be able to find translated copies of ancillary materials online.

2. If you are using a word problem, simplify the linguistic complexity of the problem, and rephrase it so that English learners can more readily understand the important information. Simplifying the language does not mean watering down the content. In essence, your English learners should be working on the same problems as native English speakers, but with some of the language simplified to make navigating the problem a little easier for them. For example:

Original problem: When you arrive on Monday morning, you observe a snail making its way up the wall of your cabin. Each day, it carefully works its way 30 inches up the wall. At night, though, it slips back down 12 inches. The cabin wall is 9 feet high. If the snail started on Monday, will it reach the top of the cabin wall before you leave on Friday afternoon?

Simplified problem: When you get to school on Monday morning, you see that a snail has climbed up the wall of the building. Each day, it climbs 30 inches up the wall. At night, it slips back down 12 inches. The wall is 9 feet high. If the snail started climbing on Monday, will it reach the top of the wall before you leave school on Friday?

3. Have students work together to understand the problem, and cross out any unnecessary vocabulary. They then try to solve the problem for a few minutes individually. After the students' initial attempt, ask them to write a sentence explaining their thinking and the steps they followed to attempt to solve the problem.

4. Students share their thinking and, using what they learn from each other, now work together as a whole class to solve the problem.

5. When they have arrived at a solution, they need to show their work and write a few sentences explaining how they know their answer is mathematically correct. You can provide sentence frames for students to use in writing down how they know their answer is correct. These frames can be used as long as students feel they need them. Pairs or groups are then asked to share their solutions and read their mathematical reasoning. If this makes some students anxious, you can begin by having them share their solutions in small groups first.

The interaction that takes place during group processing will no doubt take time to build, particularly if students are not used to working in this way. If this is the case in your class, follow this process with the whole group first so that students will know what to do during each phase of the problem-solving process.

In the early elementary grades, this process takes place with the whole group, with the teacher directing each step and writing the students' explanations. By the end of first grade, students should be able to take on more of this process themselves.

Other Strategies

Use as many strategies as possible for making content comprehensible during instruction — for example:

- *Use real-world examples when possible.* Try to reinforce the concepts you are teaching with examples that students can relate to or picture. Use examples from their lives, and talk students through the problems.

- *Use think-alouds to explain your reasoning.* Talk through the solution of problems so that students can hear what should be happening in their minds.

- *Use manipulatives purposefully.* Manipulatives can be a great help with teaching concepts and vocabulary. For example, some teachers use red and blue cubes when teaching the concept of negative numbers. Students use the blue cubes as negative numbers and red cubes as positive numbers. When solving a problem like $-3 + 2 =$ _____, the students physically put down 3 blue cubes and 2 red cubes. They can visually see that they have more negative cubes, so the answer will be negative. Students then remove pairs of cubes—one blue and one red—until they no longer have pairs left. In this case, the one remaining blue cube is the answer: -1. Using manipulatives in this way not only helps students understand the concept of negative but also helps them see how integers work when they add positive and negative numbers.

- *Translate words into pictures and pictures into number sentences.* Teach students how to draw a picture that helps them see the problem, and then turn their picture into a number sentence or equation. This process can be modeled by the teacher during think-alouds.

- *Provide objects, graphic representations, gestures, and other visual cues.* Working with images and visual cues helps English learners understand key mathematical vocabulary. Encourage students to draw their own visual cues as well. One teacher created a three-part word wall for key vocabulary, definitions written by students in their own words, and images or visual cues such as the symbols for multiplication.[12]

- *In the elementary grades, practice problem solving with everyday events.* Use opportunities presented within the course of the day to practice using the vocabulary that English learners will encounter in problem-solving situations. For example:

  o How many more students brought their lunch today than yesterday?

  o If we started math at 10:45 and ended at 12:00, how long did we do math?

  o If we have 8 markers and 4 are red, what is the fraction of red markers?

- *Let students practice writing their own math problems.* In this way, students have the opportunity to practice using the language of mathematics by creating their own problems. After the teacher checks them, they can be put out to be solved when students complete their assignments.[13]

- *Allow students to act out problems.* This is similar to having students draw pictures in that it allows them to try to comprehend the language of the problem by performing it.

Postinstruction Strategies

Once instruction has taken place, it is important to provide opportunities for students to interact with the new learning in order for them to internalize it. Again, it is important to take into account the needs of your students and differentiate the strategy accordingly.

The Strategy: Paired Summarizing

In paired note taking, students work together to identify the most important information that they should include in their notes. English learners can be paired with other English learners, but it is also beneficial to pair native English speakers with English learners so that they can provide a positive language role model.

Paired summarizing takes place after the unit or topic has been taught. It may happen the next day as a way of allowing students an opportunity to revisit the learning and make sure they have all the pertinent information they may need. This strategy works with students at all grade levels. In the early elementary grades, teachers facilitate the process, revisiting the learning from the previous day and adding details to a class chart that summarizes the learning. From second through fifth grades, students can summarize the learning from the previous day in their math journals.

The Strategy in Action: Domains L, S, R, W, and T

1. Pair students according to their understanding of the lesson and their language acquisition levels. Write the date and goal on the board as well as a word bank that includes vocabulary from the lesson that was taught, and ask students to copy down the information in their journals.

2. For the first ten minutes of class, students work with their partners to copy down the goal, date, and the vocabulary in the word bank from the board. For example, the word bank could contain the terms *ratio equivalent* and *proportion unit*.

3. Give the students an assignment that represents the culmination of instruction over the past week. Students have been taking notes and working on defining terms; now this partner assignment requires two students to work together to define vocabulary and explain math concepts. Here is a sample assignment:

Use your notes from last week to write a summary of what we learned using a combination of vocabulary, numbers, and pictures. Students who were absent can use the words provided in the word bank and write everything you remember about each of these words from last week.

4. Partners begin to work together using their notes from the past week to write a summary of what they learned with regard to the topic. The English learner is supported in writing his or her summary by the additional information provided in the word bank. Both students can also use their past notes to complete the assignment.

5. You can also ask students to show a sample problem and solution. This requires them to work together and talk about how to solve a particular problem.

In addition, working with a partner to negotiate the meaning of the vocabulary presents more opportunities for the English learner to be engaged in meaningful language.

6. At the end of class, pairs of students are asked to share their summaries as well as sample problems, if it was required of them. Some language that you might expect to see from the example could include "You must have the same units when comparing ratios," or, "Equivalent ratios are two ratios that look different but mean the same thing." The opportunity for language learners to write a summary helps move them to their next level of understanding as well as their next level of language acquisition.

Chapter 23

Strategies for Other Content Areas

In This Chapter

- The importance of collaboration between the ESL and content-area teachers
- Teaching text features explicitly
- Prereading strategies
- Summarizing the learning

One of the most effective strategies for ensuring that English learners can access the content during content-area instruction is to combine the efforts of the content-area teacher and the ESL teacher. With their combined force, they are equipped to plan an effective ESL program.

In the ideal ELL program, ESL teachers use the ESL block to work on content-area vocabulary before that content is taught in the regular education classroom. If we consider *prior knowledge* that knowledge that students bring with them to our classrooms, then background knowledge is the knowledge we help them build when they lack rich prior knowledge. The mere act of this "front-loading" helps to build background knowledge in students who may have limited prior knowledge.

In order for this to be possible, ESL teachers must have the opportunity to meet with the regular education teachers on a scheduled basis in order to plan integrated ESL lessons that are connected to the instruction in the regular education class. This presents a few challenges.

Currently, opportunities for ESL and regular education teachers to collaborate are limited at best, and the result is that students often receive unrelated instruction in their ESL classes. In order for students to receive a cohesive, well-integrated ESL program, school leadership needs to ensure that teachers are encouraged and provided with substantial time to collaborate. Here is how this collaboration might work:

> After the regular education teachers have met to plan upcoming units of instruction, they schedule a time to meet with the ESL teachers. During that meeting, the fourth-grade regular education teachers share that during the next month, students will be learning the following material:
>
> *Language arts:* Reading informational text
>
> *Math:* Geometry—area and perimeter
>
> *Social studies:* Native Americans: Plains, Northwest Coast, and desert Indians
>
> *Science:* Habitats: oceans, deserts, plains, mountains, lakes and rivers
>
> Armed with this information, the ESL teacher begins strategically planning her upcoming ESL lessons. Her goal is to stay at least one week ahead of what the regular education teachers will be teaching.

Although front-loading content during the ESL block is a logical way to organize ESL and content instruction in a way that makes sense for students, not all schools have the resources or staff to be able to implement ESL in this way.

In the most common situation, English learners are placed in mainstream content-area classrooms with all levels of learners, including some who read below grade level. Using effective teaching strategies that help all students understand the content becomes mandatory for teachers facing these challenges. Consider these, for example:

- Pause frequently.

- Paraphrase often.

- Emphasize and repeat key ideas and vocabulary.

- Write key terms and concepts on the board.

- Use pronouns sparingly.

- Shorten and simplify sentences (but not the content).

- Increase wait time for students to process the information and come up with answers.

Teaching Text Features

English language learners need to learn about the common text features in content-area textbooks and how those features can help them understand the material. Depending on the grade level, teachers should teach text features to all students, but English learners in particular benefit from such instruction. Table 23.1, which sets out these features, can be used by teachers at all grade levels to teach students the text features of their textbooks and the function of each feature. Form 23.1 can be used as a note-taking tool by students.

Table 23.1 Text Features in Textbooks

Print features

Table of Contents	Identifies key features and the order in which they appear
Preface	Provides readers with an overview of the content in the book
Glossary	Defines words in the text
Appendix	Includes additional resources for readers
Index	Helps readers find what's in the text; topics are listed alphabetically with page numbers

Organizational aids

Titles	Identify what the section is about
Headings	Identify topics within a chapter
Glossary	Identifies key words in the text and defines them.
Sidebars	Contain additional or explanatory information
Subheadings	Help readers navigate through different sections of the text
Captions	Briefly explain the meaning behind a picture, drawing, map, graph, or something similar
Italics and bold type	Highlights that the italicized (or bold) wording is important
Bullets	Indicate key points and concepts

(Continued)

Table 23.1 Text Features in Textbooks (Continued)

Graphics and images

Photographs	Help readers see what places, people, and things they are reading about look like
Drawings and diagrams	Help the readers understand how something works
Diagrams	Help to make complex information understandable
Maps	Identify where places are in the world
Charts and tables	Summarize or compare information
Time lines	Identify when events took place

Form 23.1 Text Features Worksheet

Text Feature

How It Helps Me Understand the Information I'm Reading

Table of Contents

_____

_____

_____

Titles

_____

_____

_____

Subtitles

_____

_____

_____

Bold and italicized words

_____

_____

_____

Illustrations

_____

_____

_____

Maps

_____

_____

_____

Captions

_____

_____

_____

The Strategy: Prereading Text

Prereading is a strategy that all students can use. It helps prepare students for the content they are about to read by exposing them to the vocabulary, titles, captions, images, and other context clues that ultimately serve to provide them with a basic structure for what the learning will entail. As a result, by the time the students are asked to read the text, they have been provided with all the skills necessary to ensure success.

The Strategy in Action: Domains L, S, R, W, and T

1. In advance of the prereading assignment, divide the class into groups consisting of no more than five students each. Assign each group a portion of the text on which to focus.

2. As students prepare to read the chapter, inform them that they will be prereading the textbook today to prepare for reading the next day. The goal of the prereading assignment is for each group to be able to predict what the chapter will be about and gain enough information to formulate questions about the material. This information will help them focus their reading the next day.

3. Assign each group one of these text features:

   • Titles, headings, and subheads

   • Pictures, tables, graphs, and charts

   • Captions under the illustration, tables, graphs, and charts

   • Topic sentences

4. Ask each group to preread for its specific text features only. For example, the group that is prereading the pictures should look only at the pictures, graphs, tables, charts, and any other illustration in the chapter. Conversely, the group that is prereading the captions should not read the titles or headings in the chapter. Provide as much time as you think students will need to conduct their prereading tasks. On average, ten minutes is enough for this part of the exercise.

5. Once the students have completed the prereading, they begin filling out Form 23.2, a two-column note-taking guide. They list everything they now know or think they know, and then any questions that each piece of information might have raised for them. After working individually for a few minutes, students are given the opportunity to share their facts and questions with each other.

Form 23.2 Prereading a Text

Facts	Questions

Predictions:

_____

_____

_____

_____

_____

_____

_____

6. After the students have shared the information they've gathered as a group, ask them to make a prediction that they will share with the rest of the class. They are welcome to write more than one prediction; however, they are required to read only one. The sentence frames from reciprocal teaching for students in levels 2 and 3 found in Chapter Twenty can help scaffold the writing of the predictions.

7. Give each group the opportunity to share its predictions. Any dissenting opinions (although there really shouldn't be any in this case) can be shared at this point.

8. Record the facts and question using the SMART board or document camera. They can be referred to again and added to as students read the material the following day.

The Strategy: K-Q-L

In content areas of science, math, and social studies, students are often asked to make sense of complex information. Whereas native English speakers often struggle to comprehend complex text and concepts, English learners with limited vocabulary and literacy skills are at a real disadvantage. The following prereading strategy related to a K-Q-L chart helps students prepare for the upcoming content by accessing prior knowledge and developing questions about the content. It helps students make sense out of very complex text.

The Strategy in Action: Domains L, S, W, and T

1. The teacher begins by introducing the topic or content. Post a large version of the K-Q-L chart (Form 23.3) on the document camera, overhead, or SMART board, and give each student a copy of the form. Introduce this version particularly if students are not familiar with the expectations.

2. Have students work individually for about three minutes, jotting down anything they may already know about the content. If they are unsure of a particular fact, they should add it as a question under the Questions I Have column.

Form 23.3 K-Q-L Chart

What I Already Know	Questions I Have	What I Learned

3. After three minutes, students may stand up and meet with a partner to share what they already know and questions they have. If they encountered information new to them, they may add it to their chart. If they are unsure about this piece of knowledge, they need to formulate a question about it.

4. Students return to their seats and begin to build some collective knowledge about the topic. Student volunteers can share information they have recorded on their K-Q-L chart, as well as questions they may have about the topic.

5. At this point you can read a short book tied to the topic that may provide slightly more information than students already possess.

6. At the conclusion of the short reading, students may begin to answer some of their questions, but often the information can be structured so that it serves to provide more questions rather than answers. I consider this a teaser, as it seldom provides enough information to answer all questions (and if it does, I make sure to avoid sharing that information). The students are left not having enough content knowledge to answer their questions, which is just the motivation they need to come back tomorrow to learn more.

7. The next day, students are assigned different portions of text to read within their groups. Each group works to answer as many of their questions as possible by learning as much new information as they can. Students may volunteer to add what they learned to the larger poster.

Not all questions may be answered within the context of this assignment. In fact, students may develop new questions as a result of the reading and should be encouraged to seek the answers to those questions on their own.

Differentiation for Levels 1 and 2 English Learners

Levels 1 and 2 students can work with the teacher or another student and can use a word bank, sentence frames, and drawings to complete their chart. They can also be provided with high-interest low-readability books or books in their primary language instead of the textbook. The bottom line is helping them to access content.

The Strategy: REAP

REAP is a strategy that can be used with content-area instruction to help students read and understand text.[1] It is an acronym for the following stages of reading comprehension: read, encode, annotate, ponder.

How to Reach and Teach English Language Learners

The Strategy in Action: Domains R, W, and T

1. Students can work individually or with a partner. First, define the four stages of reading:

    R—Read the text on your own.

    E—Encode the text by putting what you read into your own words.

    A—Annotate the text by recording the main ideas, significant words, quotes, or other notes.

    P—Ponder what you read by thinking about it and talking with others, connecting what you learned to other things you've learned, and developing questions about the topic.[2]

2. Students read the text and fill in each of the sections of the graphic organizer in Form 23.4 reflecting their responses to each of the four stages.

3. Students share their notes and questions with a partner to check their comprehension. Always allow opportunities for students to check their understanding, particularly when they are reading complex text.

4. The questions generated by this process can lead the class into further study of the topic, particularly if they did not find the answers within the text.

Form 23.4 REAP Notes

Taken from *How to Reach and Teach English Language Learners* by Rachel Carrillo Syrja, copyright © 2011 by John Wiley & Sons, Inc.

R	Read the text. Record the title and author.
E	Encode the text by summarizing the text in your own words.
A	Annotate the text by writing down the main ideas, or other notes in your own words.
P	Ponder the text by talking and thinking about what you learned. Record questions that you have about the text, and share those questions with your partner.

R	E
A	**P**

How to Reach and Teach English Language Learners

Part Five Resources

Form 5R.1 My Favorite Things

Name _____

Read the lists of favorite things to do and learn about below. Put a ✓ next to the ones that you like most. If your favorites aren't listed, then just add them on the bottom. I can't wait to learn more about you!

Things I like to do:

☐ Fix things

☐ Paint or draw

☐ Listen to music

☐ Play an instrument

☐ Build things

☐ Help people

☐ Talk to my friends

☐ Write stories or plays

☐ Read books

☐ Dance or sing

☐ Do puzzles

☐ Act out plays

☐ Play outside

☐ Go for walks

Things I like to learn about:

☐ Art

☐ Different countries

☐ New languages

☐ Maps

☐ People in other parts of the world

☐ The future

☐ Animals

☐ Music

☐ Painting

☐ Photography

☐ Astronomy (stars)

Other things I like to do:

Other things I like to learn about:

Form 5R.2 Secondary Student Interest Survey

Name: _____

1. What is your favorite food?

2. Do you have a favorite book?

3. What is your favorite computer activity?

4. Do you enjoy reading?

5. What is your favorite subject in school?

6. What do you like to do for fun in your free time?

7. What kind of music do you like?

8. Do you like sports? Which is your favorite?

9. Do you have a favorite team?

10. Do you play a sport?

11. What career would you like to have?

12. What are your responsibilities when you get home from school?

Use the back of this sheet to add anything else you would like me to know about you.

Discussion Questions

1. Do content-area and ESL teachers currently work together to plan cohesive ESL instruction that front-loads content-area learning?

2. Is there a way to make that level of collaboration possible at my grade level or for my content area? How about at my entire school?

3. What strategies am I not currently using that would help make content more comprehensible for my English learners? Is there one strategy I can begin using immediately?

4. What resources do I need to implement more of these strategies in my classroom?

5. Are there other research-based strategies I can use?

6. How can I make sure that I embed opportunities for listening, speaking, reading, writing, and thinking into my teaching?

Part Six

Putting These Practices to Work

The final logical step is thinking about how these practices can work for you. What are some steps you can take to ensure that you have a high-quality program for English learners and that they are receiving the best research-based instructional strategies in every content area?

Chapter 24

How Can I Make These Practices Work for My English Learners?

A person who never made a mistake, never tried anything new.

ALBERT EINSTEIN

In This Chapter

- The research behind changing teacher practices
- Microteaching, a research-proven strategy that has positive effects on student learning

What is the best way to change instructional practice? So many of us go through our careers depending on the same tried-and-true strategies that have always seemed to work. However, many of us have found that those strategies may not be working so well as they once did, and yet we expect to see growth each year when we receive the annual test scores for our students and are disappointed and disillusioned that they don't show much improvement. But if nothing has changed in the way we teach, how do we expect to see different results? In fact, our insistence on continuing to teach in the same way we've always taught benefits neither us nor our students. In order to maximize the learning for students, it is up to us to change our practices in order to meet their needs. This chapter turns to a strategy for implementing new practices that is supportive of teachers and helps them grow as professionals.

The Strategy: Microteaching

One of the biggest issues with identifying effective professional development practices is that most studies measure a teacher's reaction to the learning, not the impact that the professional development had on student achievement. Hattie found that while professional development was likely to change teacher learning (effect size = 0.90), those effects had less of an impact on teacher behavior (effect size = 0.60) and even less of an effect on student learning (effect size = 0.42).[1] In the meta analysis that Harrison conducted, Hattie explains that while professional development increased teachers' knowledge (effect size = 1.11) and overall feelings of job satisfaction (effect size = 0.85), the effects on student outcomes were minimal.[2] At issue, then, is how we get professional development to translate into improved learning for students—in this case, specifically English learners.

While professional development had an effect size of $d = 0.62$ overall, one specific type of professional development stood out above the rest. Hattie found that microteaching had an effect size of $d = 0.88$ on student achievement, which translates to as much as two to three years of growth. *Microteaching* is a systematic process of analysis, reflective teaching, videotaping, and classroom observation, followed by debriefing and discussion about the lesson.[3] All of this happens in a nonjudgmental, nonevaluative environment that fosters growth and trust. Although this strategy is most commonly used with new teachers, it is also an effective professional development model for developing and tenured teachers.

The Strategy in Action

In order for a strategy like microteaching to be implemented effectively, there needs to be a culture of trust within a school, which may take time to nurture and develop. Teachers need to feel open in sharing their instructional practice with their colleagues. Many schools have made it common practice to have small teams of teachers observing instruction in classrooms and providing feedback to their peers. Once this culture is established, teachers begin to feel more open about sharing their practice and having their lessons videotaped for feedback purposes.

If you would like to establish this type of culture at your school, start small, and be sure that teachers know that any information gathered during these observations is nonevaluative in nature. Then make sure you honor your word. There are too many instances where administrators have made this commitment but later included the details of these formative observations in a summative evaluation. If you are a teacher and feel that you would benefit greatly from this type of job-embedded professional development, find a colleague who would be willing to work with you. Others are likely to take notice as you share your successes and improved student achievement as a result of implementing research-based instructional strategies.

Prior to the observation and videotaping of the lesson, the observer should meet with the teacher and conduct a preobservation conference. During this brief meeting, the teacher informs the observer the lesson that he or she will observe, including the strategies he or she will use and any differentiation that has been made to the content. The teacher also informs the observer of any areas of concern he or she would like to have feedback on. For example, a teacher may be concerned that not all students are actively engaged, so the observer would make a special effort to provide feedback to the teacher on student engagement.

Because microteaching involves a teacher or team of teachers observing a lesson or portion of a lesson in another classroom, teachers need to work together to schedule these events and find appropriate coverage of their classrooms during the observation. Having a roving substitute cover classes while the teams are observing is ideal, but often an administrator or other personnel can cover a class in order to save on costs. Teachers also need access to a video camera to record the lesson in action. Shoot-and-share video cameras can be used to videotape a lesson and play back the footage instantly. Most district office technology departments have audiovisual equipment available.

During the lesson, the teacher is observed and videotaped. If the observation does not take place in the teacher's actual classroom, the lesson can be conducted in a laboratory setting where students are brought in for a short period of time and the teacher conducts the lesson in this setting. Although this is not ideal, it does allow the microteaching to take place before or after school or during lunch, recess, or prep time. Of course, the ideal situation is for the teacher to be observed in his or her own classroom.

At the conclusion of the short observation, typically lasting one class period, the teachers can meet to debrief the lesson. This debriefing can take place right after the observation or scheduled for later. Either way, the teacher is provided with the videotape footage and is given the opportunity to review it and reflect on the effectiveness of the lesson and the strategies used.

The observer provides feedback and coaching to the teacher based on the findings of the observation. If the observer used a scoring guide, the scores are shared with the teacher in an effort to provide formative feedback that the teacher can apply in practice.

The teacher then reflects on the observation and makes any necessary adjustments to his or her implementation of strategies. At this point, the teacher can decide whether to have the next observation focus on the same strategy in order to examine growth or choose a different content area or strategy for the next round of observations.

Research shows that if microteaching takes hold on a campus, the results can be improved performance for both teachers and students. If this model of professional development can result in dramatic levels of improvement, why wouldn't we work to implement it at our school or district?

The foundation for microteaching to work effectively must be based on mutual respect. Rooney writes, "When teachers feel respected and supported, they find the courage to take risks and grow."[4] Ultimately, we should aim to establish this type of learning environment for both teachers and students.

Ideas for Administrators

- Begin building a culture of collaboration at your school by joining with teachers who are ready and willing to work with you.

- Build on the success you nurture with this small group. As word spreads about the positive results, soon others will be asking to be part of a microteaching team.

- Remain true to your word. If teachers were told that these observations were to be nonevaluative in nature, then be sure to not blur the lines between evaluation and formative feedback. Formative feedback is essential to the learning process, and teachers don't receive enough of it. Microteaching opens up opportunities for teachers to receive the feedback they need to grow and develop as educators.

- Build your school's capacity to spread this model by investing in the teachers who start this process with you. Develop their leadership skills, and work with them on rolling out this model to other grade-level or content-area teams. While it would be natural to think that you need to send teachers to outside training or bring in a consultant to help you, in this case, you've built the capacity within your own staff so they can now be the messengers for other interested teams. Nothing holds more credibility with teachers than their own colleagues sharing strategies that have worked in their classrooms with their shared population of students. Only if you find that your teams are unwilling to lead others should you look to outside resources.

How to Reach and Teach English Language Learners

Ideas for Teachers

- If you'd like to get a microteaching model up and running at your school, begin by finding a colleague who would be willing to implement it with you. If you are a department or grade-level chairperson, talk to your team about the possibility of working together with them. Remember to provide evidence that this strategy works. Keep in mind that, like you, your colleagues may be feeling overwhelmed, so be sure to let them know that this model requires nothing of them other than participation in the process. Always keep your administrator informed about what your team is doing. He or she will appreciate this information, and it may pique his or her interest about microteaching, particularly if your team experiences success.

- Work with your team on establishing an observation schedule. Offer to be the first person to be observed. Set up guidelines, and reinforce that these observations are purely for coaching and personal growth and that any information gathered will be kept confidential between the observer and the person being observed. Establishing confidentiality, particularly at the beginning of the process, is essential to building trust. As microteaching becomes embedded in your team's practice, teachers may begin to feel more open to sharing observations with each other as a way of promoting growth within the team.

- Build on your team's successes. Once the strategies being observed begin to show improvement in student achievement, search for other research-based strategies to implement as a team. Success breeds success, so capitalize on your team's improvements and push them to continue to grow.

- Once the team reaches a high level of confidence and trust in each other and the process, discuss the possibility of inviting another team or your administrator to join you on a microteaching observation.

- Be ready and willing to expand microteaching to other interested grade levels or content areas. Teachers are looking to implement strategies that work, and nothing holds more credibility than your team of teachers sharing their process for deepening the implementation of strategies that are proven to work with your students.

Part Six Resources

Microteaching Checklist

- [ ] Connect with interested teachers who would be willing to work with you on implementing this strategy.

- [ ] Arrange for coverage of classes. You will need to have someone cover your class while you observe the teacher. If you plan to meet after the observation for a quick debriefing, keep in mind that you will need to arrange for coverage of both classrooms.

- [ ] Schedule the microteaching preconference. During this brief meeting, share the strategy that will be observed, along with any pertinent information that will enrich the observation. For example, you may want the observer to focus on a particular element of their instruction.

- [ ] Meet immediately following the observation or at a later time for a debriefing. The conference should take place as soon as possible after the observation so that you can make any necessary adjustments to your teaching, and so the details of the lesson are clear in the observer's memory.

- [ ] You may view the video of the lesson along with the teacher who videotaped it if she or he is comfortable with that arrangement. This debriefing provides time for feedback and opportunities for the observer to pause the video and provide coaching tips as you watch the footage. Although this model can cause anxiety for the teacher being observed, it is the best model of microteaching because it allows detailed and prescriptive feedback for the teacher. Your goal should be to work up to the point where your team is comfortable with watching the video footage during the debriefing after the observation.

☐ Provide time for the teacher being observed to reflect on the strategy being observed and the feedback received during the debriefing. This reflection should include next steps in revising the implementation of the strategy.

☐ Schedule the next observation cycle at the end of each debriefing.

Discussion Questions

1. How do teachers at your school implement new strategies?

2. Do you feel that this approach is effective and has a positive impact on student achievement?

3. If not, do you think your staff would be open to trying microteaching? If not, what are their reasons for not trying it?

4. What steps can you take to foster a nurturing and safe environment for learning where teachers feel open to having observers in their classroom?

5. What steps can you take to foster trust among you and your staff? If you are a teacher, how can you foster trust with your grade-level or content-area team?

6. What steps can you take to initiate the implementation of the microteaching model at your school or grade level? Remember to start small, and build on your successes.

7. Is there a structure in place for sharing the strategies that work with other grade levels and teachers at your school?

How to Reach and Teach English Language Learners

Notes

Chapter One

1. Hattie (2009).
2. Padolsky (2006).
3. Thomas and Collier (1997).
4. D. Reeves (2010).
5. Collier and Thomas (1989).
6. Cummins (2000).
7. Thomas and Collier (1997).
8. Cummins (1996).
9. Ruiz-de-Velasco and Fix (2000).
10. Fix and Capps (2005).
11. Reyes and Moll (2004).
12. Capps et al. (2004).
13. Espinosa, Laffey, and Whittaker (2006).

Chapter Two

1. Fix and Capps (2005).
2. Thomas and Collier (1999).
3. Fix and Capps (2005).
4. Fix and Capps (2005).
5. Clewell, de Cohen, and Murray (2005).
6. Clewell, de Cohen, and Murray (2005).
7. Spencer and Reno (2009).
8. Spencer and Reno (2009).
9. Cleveland (2011).
10. August and Hakuta (1997).

Chapter Three

1. Olsen (2010).
2. Olsen (2010).
3. Olsen (2010).
4. Olsen (2010).
5. Olsen (2010).

Chapter Four

1. Espinosa and López (2007).
2. McLaughlin (1984).
3. Reyes and Moll (2004).
4. Tabors and Snow (1994).
5. Tabors (1997).
6. McLaughlin, Blanchard, and Osanai (1995, pp. 3–4).
7. García (2003).

Part One Resources

1. This section is adapted from Olson (2010).

Chapter Five

1. Abedi (2008).
2. Abedi (2008).
3. Short and Fitzsimmons (2007).
4. Thomas and Collier (1997).
5. Cummins and Genzuk (1991).
6. Thomas and Collier (1997).
7. Thomas and Collier (1997).
8. Gandara, Maxwell-Jolly, and Driscoll (2005).
9. Thomas and Collier (1997).
10. Asher (2009)

Chapter Six

1. Asher (2009).

Chapter Seven

1. Stiggins, Arter, Chappuis, and Chappuis (2006).
2. Ainsworth (2003a).
3. Ainsworth (2006).

Chapter Eight

1. O'Connor (2010); D. Reeves (2011).
2. Kennelly and Monrad (2007).
3. Snow (2002, p. 87).
4. Guskey (2000, p. 7).
5. Darling-Hammond (2010, p. 30).

Part Two Resources

1. González, Moll, and Amanti (2005).

Chapter Ten

1. Krashen and Terrell (1983).
2. Krashen (1981, pp. 6–7).
3. Krashen and Terrell (1983).

Chapter Eleven

1. Henderson and Mapp (2002, p. 12).
2. Goodwin (2000).
3. Epstein et al. (2002).
4. Barr and Parrett (2007).
5. Barr and Parrett (2007).

Chapter Twelve

1. Ladson-Billings (1995).
2. Trueba (1999, p. 260).
3. Moll, Amanti, Neff, and González (2001, p. 133).
4. González, Moll, and Amanti (2005).
5. Kier Lopez (2007).
6. Kier Lopez (2007).
7. J.R. Reeves (2006).
8. Larsen-Freeman and Long (1991).
9. Cummins (1979).

Chapter Thirteen

1. Hattie (2009, p. 18).
2. Editorial Projects in Education (2009).
3. D. Reeves (2006).
4. Ainsworth (2006).
5. Ainsworth (2003b).

Chapter Fourteen

1. Tierney and Shanahan (1991).
2. Tierney and Shanahan (1991).

Chapter Fifteen

1. Krashen (1981, 1985).
2. Haynes (2010).
3. Krashen (1985 p. 26).
4. Ellis (1992). This approach certainly warrants more study and further exploration.

Chapter Sixteen

1. Asher (1982).
2. Asher (2009).
3. Cummins (1986).
4. Krashen (1987, p. 23).

Chapter Seventeen

1. Echevarria, Vogt, and Short (2010).
2. CATESOL (1992).
3. Education Alliance (2006).

Chapter Eighteen

1. Bishop (2010).
2. Spillett (2008).
3. Haynes (2004).

Chapter Nineteen

1. Hattie (2009); Marzano (2001).
2. Hattie (2009, pp. 7–8).
3. Hattie (2009); Marzano (2001).

Chapter Twenty

1. García (1991); Verhoeven (1990).
2. Goldenberg (1999).
3. Scarcella (2002).
4. Hakuta, Goto Butler, and Witt (2000).
5. Thomas and Collier (1997).
6. Kinsella, Stump, and Feldman (2010).
7. Hattie (2009).
8. Gersten et al. (2007).
9. Gersten et al. (2007).
10. Robb (1996).
11. Celedón-Pattichis (2003).

12. Taba (1967).
13. Dole, Duffy, Roehler, and Pearson (1991).
14. Palincsar and Brown (1986).
15. Carter (1997).
16. Palincsar and Brown
17. Palincsar and Klenk (1991).
18. Hattie (2009).
19. Hart and Risley (1995).
20. Snow, Burns, and Griffin (1998).
21. Feldman and Kinsella (2005).
22. Dutro and Moran (2003); Gersten and Baker (2000); Scarcella (1996).
23. Dutro and Moran (2003); Fillmore and Snow (2000).
24. Feldman and Kinsella (2005).
25. Cunningham and Stanovich (1998); Nagy, Herman, and Anderson (1985).
26. Beck, McKeown, and Kucan (2002); Stahl and Fairbanks (1986).
27. Edwards, Font, Baumann, and Boland (2004); Graves (2000).
28. Nagy and Scott (2000); Feldman and Kinsella (2005).
29. Anderson (1996).
30. Fountas and Pinnell (2001).

Chapter Twenty-One

1. Dyson and Freedman (1991); Graves (1975); Hillocks (1984, 1987).
2. Graves (1975, 1983).
3. D. Reeves (2008).
4. Hillocks (1984, 1987).
5. Freedman, Dyson, Flower, and Chafe (1995).
6. Hillocks and Smith (1991).
7. Hillocks (1984, 1987).
8. Cooper (1993).
9. Tierney and Shanahan (1991).
10. D. Reeves (2006).
11. Allen (2004).

Chapter Twenty-Two

1. Khisty (1993).
2. Khisty (1993).
3. Khisty (1993).
4. O'Malley and Chamot (1990, p. 52).
5. Chamot (1982).
6. O'Malley and Chamot (1990).

7. Matthews, Carpenter, Lindquist, and Silver (1984).
8. Khisty (1997).
9. Van de Walle and Lovin (2006).
10. Halliday (1975); Cuevas (1984).
11. Ainsworth and Christinson (2006).
12. Robertson (2009).
13. Brenner (1994).

Chapter Twenty-Three

1. Eanet and Manzo (1976).
2. Adapted from Allen (2004).

Chapter Twenty-Four

1. Hattie (2009).
2. Harrison (1980); Hattie (2009).
3. Hattie (2009).
4. Rooney (2010, p. 85).

Definitions and Key Terminology

The commonly used terms regarding English language learners that follow describe students who are learning to understand, speak, read, and write in English. In this book, I use *English language learner* (ELL) to refer to students who are acquiring English.

Whatever terminology is used at a particular district or school, it is imperative that it be consistent. More important than using the same vocabulary is ensuring that we are all consistent in what we mean when we use a particular term. The educational environment is riddled with strategies, terminology, and initiatives. It is both an exciting and stressful time in which to be a teacher—exciting, because we know more about what good instruction looks like than we ever have before, and stressful, because the stakes are higher than they have ever been before. The current environment requires us to be crystal clear about what we mean by the terminology we use in our daily practice. The definitions that follow, all taken from reliable sources, by no means represent the multiple meanings that many of these terms have come to represent. For that reason, it is important not only for all staff members to agree on using a consistent terminology but also that we mean the same things when we use these terms in conversations about ELLs.

Adequate Yearly Progress (AYP). According to the No Child Left Behind (NCLB) Act, annual progress must be based on each state's academic standards and is measured primarily by state assessments. Under Title I of the NCLB Act, ELLs must be tested, to the extent practicable, in the language and form most likely to yield accurate results for them.

Affective filter. The affective filter theory addresses the role that emotions such as anxiety, motivation, and self-confidence have on a student's acquisition of language. A high affective filter can be thought of as a wall that students who feel high levels of anxiety may put up. ELLs must have a low affective filter in order to learn English. The lower the anxiety level, the lower the filter. The more comfortable students are in their school environment, the more likely it is that they will acquire a new language. The best environment for acquiring a second language mimics the environment in which most of us acquired our first language: an accepting and nurturing environment in which students are encouraged to produce language at their own pace. In contrast, a high affective filter will result in high levels of anxiety, which will have a negative impact on the acquisition of a second language.

Annual measurable achievement objectives (AMAO). According to Title III of the NCLB Act, these are targets set by each state for English-language-proficiency attainment. Whether a school's ELL subgroup meets these targets contributes to the calculation of its Adequate Yearly Progress. It is important for all teachers who work with ELLs to be aware of what these growth targets are.

Basic interpersonal communication skills (BICs). The language skills needed for everyday personal and social communication. ELL students usually need from one to three years to develop this social language completely. BICS are not necessarily related to academic success.

Basic Inventory of Natural Language (BINL). An assessment designed to measure oral language proficiency in students in grades K–12 whose first language is not English. Often it is used to help place or even redesignate ELLs to mainstream classes. *See* Redesignation.

Bicultural. A term that refers to individuals who have cultural literacy in two cultures. ELLs are bicultural because they experience a different culture at home than at school. English learners as well as many native English speakers may be bicultural. It is important to recognize the many cultures represented within school and district communities so that parents and students feel a sense of pride in their cultural heritage. Biculturalism also brings with it challenges for students, who must be able to switch between languages and cultures depending on the circumstances.

Bilingual. A term that describes a person who speaks more than one language. *Bilingual* is not the same as *biliterate*.

Bilingual education. An educational program or methodology for ELLs in which differing amounts of instruction are provided in the student's native language. There are several models of bilingual education. *Bilingual early-exit programs,* seen mostly at the elementary level, refers to a program in which students receive primary language support, mostly in reading, for two to three years and then are quickly transitioned to a mainstream classroom. *Bilingual late-exit programs* allow students to acquire the second language at a more natural rate of five to seven years. Students remain in the bilingual program for several years and continue to receive 40 percent of their instructional day in the primary language even after they have been redesignated. Late-exit programs have been shown to have the highest lasting impact on student achievement. In *dual-immersion programs,* ELLs learn along with native English speakers. Instruction takes place in both English and a second language. Students remain in these programs throughout elementary school and may even continue the program in middle and high school. The goal is for every student to be bilingual. These programs are referred to as *two-way immersion* or *two-way bilingual. See* Redesignation.

Bilingual, early exit. See Bilingual education.

Bilingual, late exit. See Bilingual education.

Bilingualism. Refers to the use of two languages by a student or a community. *Additive bilingualism* is the outcome when a student acquires a second language without detriment to the first language. Students are able to maintain their primary language. *Subtractive bilingualism* refers to when the second language is acquired at the cost of the primary language; that is, the second language ultimately replaces the first language.

Biliterate. Students who are fully literate in two languages: they can read, write, and speak fluently in two languages. A widely held belief is that ELLs should leave the school system being perfectly biliterate.

Cognitive academic language proficiency (CALP). The language associated with native language literacy and cognitive development. These are the language skills needed to undertake academic tasks in the mainstream classroom. It includes content-specific vocabulary. It may take students from five to seven years to develop CALP skills. CALP developed in the first language contributes to the development of CALP in the second language.

Comprehensible input. This implies that the language, written or spoken, being used to teach the student is comprehensible. This does not imply that the concepts being taught should be simplified, but rather refers to the language being used to teach the concepts.

Content-based English as a Second Language. The goal for this instruction is to teach ELLs both English and content knowledge; in other words, content is the vehicle for teaching the English language. Some schools erroneously take this to mean that content areas such as science or social studies can replace ESL instruction.

Core content. This term refers to all of the content outside English language development instruction: math, science, social studies, history, geography, language arts, biology, and others.

Culturally responsive teaching. Recognizes and reinforces the importance of including students' cultural backgrounds in all aspects of learning (Ladson-Billings, 1994). Also referred to as *culturally responsive pedagogy* or *culturally relevant pedagogy*.

Dual immersion. *See* Bilingual education.

English as an Additional Language (EAL). A content area consisting of the structures and patterns of the English language.

English as a New Language learner (ENL). The term used by the National Board for Professional Teaching Standards to refer to English language learners.

English as a Second Language (ESL). A widely used term for teaching the structures and patterns of the English language. It typically focuses on language as opposed to content, although content-based ESL programs also exist. Although this term and similar others (for example, *English language development*) are typically used to describe English development programs, they may also be used to describe the students themselves. In the elementary grades, ESL is typically a pull-out or push-in model. In middle and high school, ESL becomes its own course. For consistency of terminology, this book always uses *ESL. See* English as a Second Language pull-out; English as a Second Language pull-in.

English as a Second Language pull-out. ELLs are pulled out of their regular mainstream classrooms for a minimum of thirty minutes a day to receive ESL instruction.

English as a Second Language push-in. The ESL teacher comes into the mainstream classroom to support the mainstream teacher and work with ELLs for at least thirty minutes every day.

English as a Second Language teachers. Teachers who are credentialed in their state for providing instruction in English as a Second Language.

English for Speakers of Other Languages (ESOL). A content area designed specifically for ELLs to learn the structures and patterns of the English language. Sometimes used in middle and high schools to refer to ESL instruction. *See* English as a Second Language.

English immersion. A program for ELLs available in some states in which they receive at least 50 percent of their instruction in their primary language. The goal is to produce students who are literate in both their native language and English. Students who are enrolled in these programs should also receive ESL instruction.

Exit criteria. The criteria established to determine when a student has gained proficiency in English, can be redesignated or reclassified as no longer requiring ESL instruction, and is ready to move to mainstream classes. *See* Redesignation.

Fluent English proficient (FEP). A term used to refer to an ELL who has been redesignated. These students maintain their FEP status and are never considered English-only or native English speakers. *See* Redesignation.

Home Language Survey. A survey provided to all families on registering for school. Its primary function is to help identify the students who need to be assessed for language proficiency. It also provides the school with information regarding families who speak a language other than English at home.

Inclusion. An education model in which general education, special education, or bilingual and ESL teachers work collaboratively in team teaching. In this model, the students remain in the mainstream class for instruction, as opposed to being pulled out and taught separately.

Inclusive education. All students in a school, regardless of their cultural or linguistic background and any strengths or weaknesses they may have in any area, are accepted as part of the school community.

IDEA proficiency tests (IPT). In accordance with the Individuals with Disabilities Education Act (IDEA), the IPT is a battery of tests for ELLs in grades K–12. The results can be used to place and redesignate ELLs. *See* Redesignation.

L1. Refers to the primary language a student speaks.

L2. Refers to the second, or target, language for a student.

Language Assessment Battery (LAB). Tests used to identify language proficiency levels. The results can also be used to place and redesignate ELLs. *See* Redesignation.

Language Assessment Scales (LAS). A battery of tests for ELLs in grades K–12 that can be used to place and redesignate ELLs. *See* Redesignation.

Language-minority students. The term used to refer to ELLs in federal education legislation. States and districts in which ELLs are not a minority group do not use this term.

Language proficiency levels. The stages that each English learner progresses through in becoming proficient in English.

Linguistically and culturally diverse (LCD). A term used to refer to ELLs.

Limited English proficient (LEP). A term used to describe a student's ability in English. Its use has been slowly discontinued mainly because of its negative connotations.

Long-term English learners (LTELs). A relatively new term used to describe ELLs who do not reach language proficiency in English. Many times these students have been in U.S. schools for more than six years and have not reached proficiency in English.

Mainstream classrooms. Classrooms populated predominantly by native English speakers or, at least, fluent L2 speakers of English. The curriculum is taught entirely in English and is not typically modified for limited-English-proficient students. Mainstream teachers teach grade-level content and move through instruction at a regular pace.

Mainstream teachers. Teachers other than the ESL teacher who have ELLs in their content-area classes. They may not hold the appropriate certification for planning instruction for ELLS and have had minimal professional development in working with these students.

Newcomer program. A temporary and intensive language development program in which ELLs new to the United States receive survival English skills consisting mostly of basic interpersonal communication skills that will ensure that the student will have a smooth transition into the appropriate English learner program. An effective newcomer program has a culturally responsive curriculum. *See* Basic interpersonal communication skills (BICs).

Non-English-proficient (NEP). Students who are in the initial stages of learning English or have not yet begun acquiring English.

Potentially English proficient (PEP). Students whose primary language is other than English, who are from different cultural and/or ethnic backgrounds, and who have the potential for becoming English proficient.

Primary or home language other than English (PHLOTE). A term used to refer to students.

Reclassification. See Redesignation.

Redesignation. Occurs when a student is ready to move into a mainstream class. This typically happens when he or she meets a combination of criteria, such as passing the state standardized proficiency test or scoring intermediate or advanced on the state English language proficiency test. Each local education agency is required to determine its own redesignation criteria.

Secondary Level English Proficiency Test (SLEP). Published by ETS, this test is intended for secondary students in grades 7 through 12 whose first language is not English. It consists of a listening comprehension section and a reading comprehension section. The SLEP is most often used to determine an initial ELL language acquisition level.

Sheltered instruction. The term used to refer to instruction in English for ELLs at the speech emergence stage of language acquisition and above that is scaffolded to make the content comprehensible. *See* Specially designed academic instruction in English.

Silent period. A period of time during which a newcomer is unable or unwilling to speak in the second language. Nearly all students go through a silent period, which can be as short as six months and as long as a year.

Specially designed academic instruction in English (SDAIE). A term used most prevalently in California that is basically synonymous with *sheltered instruction*. It refers to content-area instruction in English that is specially designed to be comprehensible to ELLs. A requirement is that students be at the speech emergence level of proficiency in English to benefit from SDAIE or sheltered instruction.

Teachers of English to Speakers of Other Languages (TESOL). A global association of teachers who work with ELLs. It encompasses a network of approximately fifty-two thousand members worldwide. The TESOL Web site contains numerous resources, including journals and research findings. Local schools and districts sometimes use this term to refer to their ESOL teachers. This term has also been taken to mean teaching English to speakers of other languages.

Test of English as a Foreign Language (TOEFL). One of the most used English assessments for ELLs entering a university.

Title I of the NCLB Act. Provides funding to schools to raise the performance of disadvantaged students.

Title III of the NCLB Act. Provides funding to schools to ensure that ELLs and immigrant children attain English proficiency and develop high levels of academic achievement in core content areas.

Total physical response (TPR). A language acquisition method developed by James Asher in the 1970s in which students respond to commands that require physical movements. This method of language learning allows a long period of listening and developing comprehension before production of the language can take place.

Woodcock-Muñoz Language Survey. An assessment designed for pre-K to adult students whose first language is not English. It assesses a student's cognitive and academic language proficiency.

References

Abedi, J. (2008, Fall). Classification system for English language learners. Educational measurement: *Issues and Practice, 27*(3), 17–31.

Ainsworth, L. (2003a). *Power standards: Identifying the standards that matter the most.* Denver, CO: Lead and Learn Press.

Ainsworth, L. (2003b). *"Unwrapping" the standards.* Englewood, CO: Advanced Learning Press.

Ainsworth, L. (2006). *Common formative assessments: How to connect standards-based instruction and assessment.* Denver, CO: Lead and Learn Press.

Ainsworth, L., & Christinson, J. (2006). *Five easy steps to a balanced math program.* Denver, CO: Lead and Learn Press.

Allen, J. (2004). *Tools for teaching content literacy.* Portland, ME: Stenhouse.

Allydog.com. (2011). *Psychology glossary.* Retrieved from http://www.education.com/definition/effect-size/

Anderson, R. C. (1996). Research foundations to support wide reading. In Creany, V. (Ed.), *Promoting reading in developing countries,* (pp. 44–77). Newark, DE: International Reading Association.

Asher, J. (1982). *The total physical response approach: Innovative approaches to language teaching.* Rowley, MA: Newbury House.

Asher, J. J. (2009). The total physical response review of the evidence. *Total Physical Response World.* Retrieved November 7, 2010, from http://www.tpr-world.com/review_evidence.pdf

August, D., & Hakuta, K. (1997). *Improving schooling for language-minority children: A research agenda.* Washington, DC: National Academies Press.

Barr, R. D., & Parrett, W. H. (2007). *The kids left behind: Catching up the underachieving children of poverty.* Bloomington, IN: Solution Tree.

Beck, I. L., McKeown, M. G., & Kucan, L. (2002). *Bringing words to life: Robust vocabulary instruction.* New York: Guilford Press.

Beers, K. (2003). *Why kids can't read: What teachers can do.* Portsmouth, NH: Heinemann.

Bishop, B. (2010). *Accelerating academic achievement for English language learners training manual.* Denver, CO: Lead and Learn Press.

Brenner, M. E. (1994). Development of mathematical communication in problem solving groups by language minority students. *Bilingual Research Journal, 22,* 214–244.

Capps, R., Fix, M., Murray, J., Ost, J., Passel, J. S., & Herwantoro, S. (2005). *The new demography of America's schools: Immigration and the No Child Left Behind Act.* Washington, DC: Urban Institute. Retrieved November 26, 2010, from http://www.urban.org/UploadedPDF/311230_new_demography.pdf

Carter, C. J. (1997). Why reciprocal teaching? *Educational Leadership, 54*(6), 64–68.

CATESOL. (1992). *Position statement on specially-designed academic instruction in English (sheltered instruction).* Retrieved March 13, 2010, from http://www.catesol.org/shelter.html

Celedón-Pattichis, S. (2003). Constructing meaning: Think-aloud protocols of ELLs on English and Spanish word problems. *Educators for Urban Minorities, 2*(2), 74–90.

Chamot, A. U. (1982). *Towards a functional ESL curriculum in the elementary school.* Rosslyn, VA: National Clearinghouse for Bilingual Education.

Cleveland, K. P. (2011) *Teaching boys who struggle in school: Strategies that turn underachievers into successful learners.* Alexandria, VA: ASCD.

Clewell, B. C., de Cohen, C., & Murray, J. (2005). *Profile of US elementary schools: LEP concentration and school capacity.* Washington, DC: Urban Institute.

Collier, V. P. (1988). *The effect of age on acquisition of a second language for school.* Washington, DC: National Clearinghouse for English Language Acquisition. Retrieved July 31, 2010, from http://www.thomasandcollier.com/Downloads/1988_Effect-of-Age-on_Acquisition-of_L2-for-School_Collier-02aage.pdf

Collier, V. P., & Thomas, W. P. (1989). How quickly can immigrants become proficient in school English? *Journal of Educational Issues of Language Minority Students, 1*(4), 26–38.

Cooper, J. D. (1993). *Literacy: Helping children construct meaning* (2nd ed.). Boston: Houghton Mifflin.

Cuevas, G. (1984). Mathematics learning in English as a second language. *Journal for Research in Mathematics Education, 15,* 134–144.

Cummins, J. (1979). Language, power, and pedagogy: Bilingual children in the crossfire. *Language Policy, 1*(2), 193–195.

Cummins, J. (1996). *Negotiating identities: Education for empowerment in a diverse society.* Los Angeles: California Association for Bilingual Education.

Cummins, J., & Genzuk, M. (1991). "Analysis of final report longitudinal study of structured English immersion strategy, early-exit and late-exit transitional bilingual education programs for language-minority students," *California Association for Bilingual Education Newsletter* 13, no. 5 (1991).

Cunningham, A. E., & Stanovich, K. E. (1998). What reading does for the mind. *American Educator, 22*(1–2), 8–15.

Darling-Hammond, L. (2010). *The flat world and education: How America's commitment to equity will determine our future.* New York: Teachers College Press.

Dole, J. A., Duffy, G. G., Roehler, L. R., & Pearson, P. D. (1991). Moving from the old to the new: Research on reading comprehension instruction. *Review of Educational Research, 61*(2), 239–264.

Dutro, S., & Moran, C. (2003). Rethinking English language instruction: An architectural approach. In G. Garcia (Ed.), *English learners: Reaching the highest level of English literacy.* Newark, DE: International Reading Association.

Dyson, A. H., & Freeman, S. W. (1991). Writing. In J. Flood, J. M. Jensen, D. Lapp, & J. R. Squire (Eds.), *Handbook of research on teaching the English language arts* (pp. 754–774). New York: Macmillan.

Eanet, M., & Manzo, A. (1976). R.E.A.P.—A strategy for improving reading/writing study skills. *Journal of Reading, 19,* 647–652.

Echevarria, J., Vogt, M. E., & Short, D. (2010). *The SIOP model for teaching mathematics to English learners.* Needham Heights, MA: Allyn & Bacon.

Editorial Projects in Education. (2009). Diplomas count 2009: Broader horizons: The challenge of college readiness for all students. *Education Week, 28*(34).

Education Alliance. (2006). Sheltered instruction. Available at http://www.alliance.brown.edu/tdl/tl-strategies/mc-principles.shtml

Edwards, E. C., Font, G., Baumann, J. F., & Boland, E. (2004). Unlocking word meanings. In J. F. Baumann & E. J. Kame'enui (Eds.), *Vocabulary instruction: From research to practice* (pp. 159–176). New York: Guilford Press.

Ellis, R. (1992). *Second language acquisition and language pedagogy.* Clevedon, UK: Multilingual Matters.

Epstein, J. L., Sanders, M. G., Simon, B. S., Salinas, K., Clark, J., Rodriguez, N., et al. (2002). *School, family, and community partnerships: Your handbook for action*. Thousand Oaks, CA: Corwin.

Espinosa, L., Laffey, J., & Whittaker, T. (2006). *Language minority children analysis: Focus on technology use* (Final Report). Washington, D.C.: Cooperation in Research and Education in Science and Technology (CREST)/National Center for Education (NCES).

Espinosa, L., & López, M. L., (2007). *Assessment considerations for young English language learners across different levels of accountability*. Philadelphia: Pew Charitable Trust.

Feldman, K., & Kinsella, K. (2005). *Narrowing the language gap: The case for explicit vocabulary instruction*. New York: Scholastic. Retrieved July 31, 2010, from http://teacher.scholastic.com /products/authors/pdfs/Narrowing_the_Gap.pdf

Fillmore, L. W. & Snow, C. E. (2000). *What teachers need to know about language*. Retrieved September 9, 2010, from http://www.cal.org/ericcll/teachers/teachers.pdf

Fix, M. E., & Capps, R. (2005). *Immigrant children, urban schools, and the No Child Left Behind Act*. Washington, DC: Migration Policy Institute. Retrieved November 26, 2010, from http://www .migrationinformation.org/usfocus/display.cfm?ID=347

Fountas, I. C., & Pinnell, G. S. (2001). *Guiding readers and writers grades 3–6 : Teaching comprehension, genre, and content literacy*. Portsmouth, NH: Heinemann.

Freedman S. W., Dyson, A. H., Flower, L., & Chafe, W. (1991). *Research in writing: Past, present and future*. Cleveland, OH: Center for the Study of Writing.

Gandara, P., Maxwell-Jolly, J., & Driscoll, A. (2005). *Listening to teachers of English language learners: A survey of California teachers' challenges, experiences, and professional development needs*. Regents of the University of California, Center for the Future of Teaching and Learning.

Garcia, G. E. (1991). Bilingualism, second language acquisition, and the education of Chicano language minority students. In R. R. Valencia (Ed.), *Chicano school failure and success: Research and policy agendas for the 1990s*. New York: Falmer.

García, G. E. (2003). The reading comprehension development and instruction of English-language learners. In A. P. Sweet & C. E. Snow (Eds.), *Rethinking reading comprehension* (pp. 30–50). New York: Guilford Press.

Gersten, R., & Baker, S. (2000). What we know about effective instructional practices for English-language learners. *Exceptional Children, 66*, 454–470.

Gersten, R., Baker, K. S., Shanahan, T., Linan-Thompson, S., Collins, P., & Scarcella, R. (2007). *Effective literacy and English language instruction for English learners in the elementary grades*. Washington, DC: National Center for Education Evaluation and Regional Assistance, U.S. Department of Education.

Goldenberg, C. (1999). Teaching English language learners: What the research does—and does not—say. *American Educator, 32*(2), 8–23, 42–44.

González, N., Moll, L., & Amanti, C. (2005). *Funds of knowledge: Theorizing practices in households, communities, and classrooms*. Mahwah, NJ: Erlbaum.

Goodwin, B. (2000, May). *Raising the achievement of low-performing students*. Aurora, CO: Mid-Continent Research for Education and Learning. Retrieved March 13, 2010, from http://www.mcrel.org:80/topics/products/105/

Graves, D. H. (1975). An examination of the writing processes of seven-year-old children. *Research in the Teaching of English, 9*, 227–241.

Graves, D. H. (1983). *Writing: Teachers and children at work*. Exeter, NH: Heinemann.

Guskey, T. (2000). *Evaluating professional development*. Thousand Oaks, CA: Corwin Press.

Hakuta, K., Goto Butler, Y., & Witt, D. (2000). *How long does it take English learners to attain proficiency?* (Policy Report 2000–1). Santa Barbara: University of California Linguistic Minority Research Institute.

Halliday M.A.K. (1975). *Learning how to mean.* London,UK: Edward Arnold.

Harrison, A. (1980). *A language testing handbook.* London: MacMillan.

Hart, B., & Risley, T. (1995). *Meaningful differences.* Baltimore, MD: Paul H. Brookes.

Hattie, J. (2009). *Visible learning: A synthesis of over 800 meta-analyses relating to achievement.* London: Routledge.

Haynes, J. (2004). *Understanding second language terminology.* Retrieved September 2, 2010, from http://www.everythingesl.net/inservices/essential_vocab.php

Haynes, J. (2010). *Tips on communicating.* Retrieved September 2, 2010, from http://www.everythingesl.net/inservices/tipsoncommunicating.php

Henderson, A., & Mapp, K. (2002). *A new wave of evidence: The impact of school, family, and community connections on student achievement.* Austin, TX: Southwest Educational Development Laboratory.

Hillocks, G. (1984). What works in teaching composition: A meta-analysis of experimental treatment studies. *American Journal of Education, 93*(1), 133–170.

Hillocks, G. (1987). Synthesis of research on teaching writing. *Educational Leadership, 44,* 71–82.

Hillocks, G., Jr., & Smith, M. W. (1991). Grammar and usage. In J. Flood, J. M. Jensen, D. Lapp, & J. R. Squire (Eds.), *Handbook of research on teaching the English language arts* (pp. 591–603). New York: Macmillan.

Kennelly, L., & Monrad, M. (2007). *Approaches to dropout prevention: Heeding early warning signs with appropriate interventions.* Washington, DC: American Institutes for Research, National High School Center. Retrieved from www.betterhighschools.org/topics/DropoutWarningSigns.asp

Khisty, L. L. (1993). A naturalistic look at language factors in mathematics teaching in bilingual classrooms. In *Proceedings of the Third National Research Symposium on Limited English Proficient Student Issues: Focus on Middle and High School Issues.* Washington, DC: U.S. Department of Education, Office of Bilingual and Minority Language Affairs.

Kier Lopez, J. (2007). *Funds of knowledge.* University of North Carolina. Retrieved July 31, 2010, from http://www.learnnc.org/lp/editions/brdglangbarriers/939

Kinsella, K., Stump, C. S., & Feldman, K. (2010). *Language arts instruction and English language learners.* Retrieved September 12, 2010, from http://www.phschool.com/eteach/language_arts/2001_12/essay.html

Krashen, S. D. (1981). *Second language acquisition and second language learning.* Elmsford, NY: Pergamon Press.

Krashen, S. D. (1985). *The input hypothesis.* London: Longman.

Krashen, S. D. (1987). *Principles and practice in second language acquisition.* Upper Saddle River, NJ: Prentice Hall.

Krashen, S. D., & Terrell, T. D. (1983). *The natural approach: Language acquisition in the classroom.* Hayward, CA: Alemany Press.

Ladson-Billings, G. (1994). *The dreamkeepers.* San Francisco: Jossey-Bass.

Ladson-Billings, G. (1995). But that's just good teaching! The case for culturally relevant pedagogy. *Theory into Practice, 34*(3), 159–165.

Larsen-Freeman, D., & Long, M. H. (1991). *An introduction to second language acquisition research.* London: Longman.

Marzano, R. (2001). *Classroom instruction that works: Research based strategies for improving student achievement.* Alexandria, VA: Association for Supervision and Curriculum Development.

Matthews, W., Carpenter, T., Lindquist, M., & Silver, E. (1984). The Third National Assessment: Minorities and mathematics. *Journal for Research in Mathematics Education, 15,* 165–171.

McLaughlin, B. (1984). *Second language acquisition in childhood: Preschool children.* Mahwah, NJ: Erlbaum.

McLaughlin, B., Blanchard, A., & Osani, Y. (1995). *Assessing language development in bilingual preschool children.* Washington, DC: George Washington University.

Moll, L., Amanti, C., Neff, D., & Gonzales, N. (2001). Funds of knowledge for teaching: Using a qualitative approach to connect homes and classrooms. *Theory into Practice, 31,* 132–141.

Nagy, W. E., Herman, P. A., & Anderson, R. C. (1985). Learning words from context. *Reading Research Quarterly, 20,* 233–253.

National Center for Education and Statistics. (1990). *1990 Census.* Retrieved September 10, 2010, from http://nces.ed.gov/pubs98/9807.pdf

Olsen, L. (2010). *Reparable harm: Fulfilling the unkept promise for California's long term English learners.* Long Beach: Californians Together. Retrieved December 1, 2010, from http://www.calfund.org/pub_documents/reparable_harm_full_final_lo.pdf

O'Connor, K. (2009). *A repair kit for broken grades: 15 Fixes for broken grades.* Portland, OR: Educational Testing Service.

O'Malley, J. M., & Chamot, A. U. (1990). *Learning strategies in second language acquisition.* Cambridge: Cambridge University Press.

Padolsky, D. (2006). *Ask NCELA No. 1: How many school-aged English-language learners (ELLs) are there in the U.S.?* Washington, DC: U.S. Department of Education, Office of English Language Acquisition.

Palincsar, A. S., & Brown, A. L. (1986). Interactive teaching to promote independent learning from text. *Reading Teacher, 39,* 771–777.

Palincsar, A. S., & Klenk, L. (1991). Dialogues promoting reading comprehension. In B. Means, C. Chelemer, & M. S. Knapp (Eds.), *Teaching advanced skills to at-risk students* (pp. 112–140). San Francisco: Jossey-Bass.

Reading Professional Development Institute. (1999). *Focusing on results, K-3.* San Diego: California Reading and Literature Project.

Reeves, J. R. (2006). Secondary teacher attitudes toward including English language learners in mainstream classrooms. *Journal of Educational Research, 99*(3), 131–142.

Reeves, D. (2006). *The learning leader: How to focus school improvement for better results.* Alexandria, VA: ASCD.

Reeves, D. (2008). *Reframing teacher leadership.* Alexandria, VA: ASCD.

Reeves, D. (2010). *Transforming professional development into student results.* Alexandria, VA: ASCD.

Reeves, D. (2011) *Elements of grading: A guide to effective practice.* Bloomington, IN: Solution Tree Press.

Reyes, I. & Moll, L. (2005) Latinos and Bilingualism. In I. Stavans & H. Augenbraum (Eds). *Encyclopedia Latina: History, culture, and society in the United States* (pp. 520–528). New York, NY: Grolier Academic Reference.

Robb, T. (1996). E-mail keypals for language fluency. *Foreign Language Educators of New Jersey, 38*(3), 8–10.

Robertson, K. (2009). *Math instruction for English learners.* Retrieved September 9, 2010, from http://www.colorincolorado.org/article/30570

Rooney, J. (2010). Meeting teachers where they are. *Educational Leadership, 67*(5), 85–86.

Ruíz-de-Velasco, J., & Fix, M. E, (2000). *Overlooked and underserved: Immigrant students in U.S. secondary schools.* Washington, DC: Urban Institute Press.

Scarcella, R. (1996). Secondary education and second language research: ESL students in the 1990s. *CATESOL Journal, 9,* 129–152.

Scarcella, R. (2002). Some key factors affecting English learners' development of advanced literacy. In M. J. Schleppegrell & M. C. Colombi (Eds.), *Developing advanced literacy in first and second languages: Meaning with power* (pp. 209–226). Mahwah, NJ: Erlbaum.

Short, D. J., & Fitzsimmons, S. (2007). *Double the work: Challenges and solutions to acquiring language and academic literacy for adolescent English language learners.* New York: Carnegie Corporation.

Snow, C. E. (2002). *Reading for understanding: Toward an R&D program in reading comprehension.* Santa Monica, CA: Rand Corporation.

Snow, C. E., Burns, S. M., & Griffin, P. (Eds.). (1998). *Preventing reading difficulties in young children.* Washington, DC: National Academies Press.

Spencer, M. L., & Reno, R. (2009). *The benefits of racial and economic integration in our education system: Why this matters for our democracy.* Columbus, OH: Kirwan Institute for the Study of Race and Ethnicity. Retrieved September 9, 2010, from http://4909e99d35cada63e7f757471b7243be73e53e14 .gripelements.com/publications/education_integration_memo_feb2009.pdf

Spillett, A. (2008). *Strategies for teaching English Language Learners.* Retrieved June 13, 2010, from http://www2.scholastic.com/browse/article.jsp?id=3747062&FullBreadCrumb=%3Ca+href%3D% 22http%3A%2F%2Fwww2.scholastic.com%2Fbrowse%2Fsearch%2F%3FNtx%3Dmode%2Bmatchall partial%26_N%3Dfff%26Ntk%3DSCHL30_SI%26query%3DAndrea%2520Spillett%2520and%2520ESL% 26N%3D0%26Ntt%3DAndrea%2BSpillett%2Band%2BESL%22+class%3D%22endecaAll%22%3EAll+ Results%3C%2Fa%3E

Stahl, S. A., & Fairbanks, M. M. (1987). The effects of vocabulary instruction: A model-based meta-analysis. *Review of Educational Research, 56,* 72–110.

Stiggins, R. J., Arter, J. A., Chappuis, J., & Chappuis, S. (2006). *Classroom assessment for student learning: Doing it right—using it well.* Portland, OR: ETS Assessment Training Institute.

Taba, H. (1967). *Teacher's handbook for elementary social studies.* Reading, MA: Addison-Wesley.

Tabors, P. O. (1997). *One child, two languages: A guide for preschool educators of children learning English as a second language.* Baltimore, MD: Paul H. Brookes.

Tabors, P. O., & Snow, C. (1994). English as a second language in pre-schools. In F. Genesee (Ed.), *Educating second language children: The whole child, the whole curriculum, the whole community* (pp. 103–125). Cambridge: Cambridge University Press.

Thomas, W. P., & Collier, V. P. (1997). *School effectiveness for language minority students.* Retrieved August 13, 2010, from http://www.thomasandcollier.com/Downloads/1997_Thomas-Collier97.pdf

Thomas, W. P., & Collier, V. P. (1999). Accelerated schooling for English language learners. *Educational Leadership, 56*(7), 46–49. Retrieved July 31, 2010, from http://www.ascd.org /ASCD/pdf/journals/ed_lead/el199904_thomas.pdf

Tierney, R. J., & Shanahan, T. (1991). Research on the reading-writing relationship: Interactions, transactions, and outcomes. In Barr, R., Kamil, M. L., Mosenthal, P., & Pearson, P. D. (Eds.), *Handbook of reading research,* Vol. 2, (pp. 246–280). New York: Longman.

Trueba, E. (1999). *Latinos unidos: From cultural diversity to the politics of solidarity.* Lanham, MD: Rowman & Littlefield.

Van de Walle, J. A., & Lovin, L. H. (2006). *Teaching student centered mathematics.* Boston: Pearson Education.

Verhoeven, L. (1990). Acquisition of reading in a second language. *Reading Research Quarterly, 25*(2), 90–114.

Index

Index